# Elixir Functional Programming:

Harnessing the Power of Functional
Paradigms for Scalable, Concurrent, and
Resilient Applications

Ethan B.Carter

# Table of Contents

6.1 The Actor Model and Processes

6.2 Spawning and Managing Processes

6.3 Messaging Between Processes


Chapter 7: Supervisors and Fault Tolerance


7.1 The Role of Supervisors in Elixir Applications

7.2 Building Fault-Tolerant Systems

7.3 Designing Resilient Applications


Chapter 8: Scalability and Distributed Systems


8.1 Understanding Scalability in Elixir

8.2 Building Distributed Applications with Elixir

8.3 Leveraging BEAM for Concurrent Systems


PART IV: ADVANCED FUNCTIONAL
PROGRAMMING TECHNIQUES


Chapter 9: Metaprogramming with Macros


9.1 Introduction to Metaprogramming

# PART I: INTRODUCTION TO FUNCTIONAL PROGRAMMING

## Chapter 1
## Understanding Functional Programming

Functional programming is a programming paradigm that focuses on building software by composing pure functions, avoiding shared state, and utilizing immutability. Unlike imperative programming, which relies on sequences of commands to change a program's state, functional programming treats computation as the evaluation of mathematical functions.

Key principles of functional programming include:

Immutability: Data cannot be modified after it is created, ensuring consistent and predictable behavior.

Pure Functions: Functions that always produce the same output for the same input without side effects, making them easier to test and debug.

First-Class Functions: Functions are treated as values, meaning they can be assigned to variables, passed as arguments, or returned from other functions.

Declarative Nature: Focuses on what to do rather than how to do it, leading to concise and readable code.

Functional programming is particularly beneficial for tasks that require concurrency, scalability, and resilience. Languages like Elixir are designed to leverage these principles, providing developers with powerful tools to build reliable and efficient systems.

## 1.1 What is Functional Programming?

Functional programming (FP) is a programming paradigm where computation is treated as the evaluation of mathematical functions. It emphasizes the use of pure functions, immutability, and a declarative coding style. In

FP, programs are constructed by composing functions that avoid changing state and mutable data, making them predictable and easier to test.

Key characteristics of functional programming include:

Pure Functions: Functions that produce the same output for the same input without causing side effects (e.g., modifying global variables or interacting with external systems).
Immutability: Data structures cannot be changed once created, promoting consistency and reducing bugs.

First-Class and Higher-Order Functions: Functions are treated as first-class citizens, allowing them to be passed as arguments, returned from other functions, or stored in variables.

Function Composition: Combining simple functions to build more complex ones.
Declarative Style: Focuses on describing what the program should accomplish rather than how it operates, leading to more concise and readable code.

Functional programming is well-suited for modern applications requiring scalability, parallelism, and reliability, making it a popular choice in fields like web development, data processing, and distributed systems. Languages like Elixir, Haskell, and Scala embrace FP principles to build robust and efficient systems.

1.2 Core Principles of Functional Paradigms

Functional paradigms focus on simplifying code, improving predictability, and enabling scalability by adhering to a set of foundational principles. These principles distinguish functional programming (FP) from other programming paradigms and make it particularly effective for building reliable and maintainable software.

1. Immutability

Immutability ensures that data cannot be modified once created. Instead of changing existing data, new data structures are created when updates are needed. This eliminates unintended side effects and makes programs easier to debug and reason about.

2. Pure Functions

Pure functions are functions where the output depends solely on the input, with no side effects (e.g., altering global variables or interacting with external systems). This makes them predictable, testable, and reusable.

3. First-Class Functions

In FP, functions are treated as first-class citizens, meaning they can be assigned to variables, passed as arguments to other functions, or returned as results. This enables higher-order functions, which take other functions as input or return them, allowing for flexible and reusable code.

4. Declarative Programming

Functional paradigms emphasize describing what to do rather than how to do it. This declarative style leads to concise, readable code that abstracts implementation details, focusing instead on the logic of computation.

5. Function Composition

Function composition involves combining smaller, simpler functions to create more complex functionality. This modular approach promotes code reusability and separation of concerns, making it easier to maintain and scale applications.

6. Statelessness

Functional programming avoids reliance on shared state or mutable objects. Each function operates independently, improving concurrency and reducing the likelihood of bugs caused by unexpected state changes.

7. Lazy Evaluation

FP often employs lazy evaluation, where expressions are not evaluated until their results are needed. This approach optimizes performance by avoiding unnecessary computations and managing resource-intensive tasks efficiently.

By adhering to these principles, functional programming enables developers to write clean, maintainable, and scalable code. Languages like Elixir, Haskell, and Scala provide robust support for these paradigms, making them ideal for modern software development challenges.

## 1.3 Why Choose Functional Programming?

Functional programming (FP) has gained significant traction in modern software development due to its ability to solve complex problems with clean, reliable, and maintainable code. By leveraging the principles of immutability, pure functions, and declarative logic, FP offers numerous advantages for developers and organizations.

### 1. Improved Code Readability and Maintainability

FP emphasizes concise, declarative code that focuses on what a program should do rather than how it does it. This makes code easier to read, understand, and modify, reducing maintenance costs and developer onboarding time.

## 2. Enhanced Predictability and Debugging

Pure functions, a cornerstone of FP, produce consistent outputs for the same inputs and avoid side effects. This predictability simplifies debugging and testing, as developers can isolate and evaluate functions without considering external factors.

## 3. Concurrency and Parallelism

FP avoids mutable state, which eliminates race conditions and conflicts in concurrent environments. This makes FP well-suited for building highly concurrent and parallel systems, such as web servers, real-time applications, and distributed systems.

## 4. Modularity and Reusability

By composing smaller, independent functions into larger programs, FP encourages modular design. These functions can be reused across different parts of the application, saving time and effort while promoting consistency.

5. Fault Tolerance and Scalability

FP languages like Elixir, running on the BEAM virtual machine, are designed for building fault-tolerant and scalable systems. This makes FP a popular choice for industries requiring high reliability, such as telecommunications, finance, and e-commerce.

6. Ease of Testing and Debugging

Immutability and statelessness simplify testing, as functions do not depend on external state or mutable data. This reduces the complexity of unit tests and makes automated testing more efficient.

7. Aligning with Modern Software Trends

As software trends like microservices, cloud computing, and distributed systems grow, FP's principles align naturally with these paradigms. Functional languages help developers write resilient, efficient, and maintainable code for these modern architectures.

8. Long-Term Benefits

While FP may have a steeper learning curve compared to other paradigms, its benefits in scalability, reliability, and reduced technical debt outweigh the initial investment. It equips teams to handle growing application complexity effectively.

Choosing functional programming is not just about adopting a new paradigm—it's about embracing a methodology that enables developers to build robust, efficient, and future-ready applications.

## Chapter 2
## Getting Started with Elixir

Elixir is a functional, concurrent programming language designed for building scalable, fault-tolerant applications. It runs on the BEAM virtual machine, which powers Erlang, making it ideal for distributed and real-time systems. Elixir's modern syntax, developer-friendly tools, and seamless concurrency support have made it a popular choice for applications like web development and telecommunications.

Key Steps to Get Started:

Install Elixir

Download and install Elixir from the official website or use package managers like Homebrew (macOS) or apt (Linux).

bash
Copy code
brew install elixir  # macOS

sudo apt-get install elixir  # Linux

Set Up Your Environment

Use Elixir's interactive shell, iex, to write and test code quickly.

```bash
Copy code
iex  # Start the Elixir shell
```

Understand Basic Syntax

Learn Elixir's fundamental concepts, such as pattern matching, immutability, and modules. For example:

```elixir
Copy code
defmodule Greeter do
  def greet(name), do: "Hello, #{name}!"
end
IO.puts Greeter.greet("World")  # Output: Hello, World!
```

Learn Functional Programming Basics

Explore Elixir's support for pure functions, immutability, and higher-order functions to understand its functional programming nature.

Explore the Ecosystem

Familiarize yourself with Elixir's ecosystem, including the Phoenix framework for web development, Ecto for database interactions, and Hex for managing dependencies.

Elixir combines the robustness of Erlang with modern syntax, making it an excellent choice for developers looking to build high-performance, scalable systems.

2.1 Overview of Elixir

Elixir is a dynamic, functional programming language designed for building scalable, maintainable, and fault-tolerant applications. Developed by José Valim in 2011, Elixir is built on top of the Erlang virtual machine

(BEAM), inheriting Erlang's powerful concurrency and distributed system capabilities while offering a modern and developer-friendly syntax.

Key Features of Elixir:

Functional Paradigm

Elixir embraces functional programming principles like immutability, pure functions, and declarative code, enabling developers to write clean, concise, and maintainable applications.

Concurrency and Scalability

Elixir leverages the BEAM virtual machine's lightweight process model, making it highly efficient for handling thousands or even millions of concurrent tasks. This makes it ideal for real-time systems, messaging platforms, and high-traffic web applications.

Fault Tolerance

Inspired by Erlang, Elixir is designed for reliability. Features like supervisors and the actor model allow applications to recover gracefully from failures, making it suitable for mission-critical systems.

Readable and Expressive Syntax

Elixir offers a Ruby-inspired syntax, making it approachable for developers new to functional programming. Its syntax prioritizes readability and developer productivity.

Extensive Ecosystem
Elixir boasts a rich ecosystem, including:

Phoenix Framework: A powerful framework for web development.

Ecto: A robust tool for database interaction.
Hex: A package manager for managing dependencies.

Tooling and Interoperability

Elixir comes with built-in tools like Mix (for project management) and IEx (an interactive shell). It is fully interoperable with Erlang, allowing developers to leverage decades of Erlang libraries and tools.

Community and Open Source

Elixir has a thriving open-source community that contributes libraries, tools, and learning resources, ensuring the language evolves and remains relevant.

Use Cases for Elixir:

Web Development: Through the Phoenix framework, Elixir powers scalable web applications.

Real-Time Systems: Ideal for messaging platforms, chat applications, and live dashboards.

Telecommunications: Used in systems requiring high reliability and uptime.
IoT and Embedded Systems: Offers scalability for connected devices.

Elixir combines modern programming concepts with the robustness of Erlang, making it a powerful choice for developers building scalable and resilient applications.

## 2.2 Installing Elixir and Setting Up Your Environment

Getting started with Elixir is straightforward and involves installing the language, setting up its tools, and preparing your environment for development.

1. Install Elixir

The easiest way to install Elixir depends on your operating system.

Windows:

Download the installer from the Elixir website.

Follow the setup wizard to install both Elixir and Erlang (required for Elixir to run).

macOS:

Use Homebrew to install Elixir:

```bash
Copy code
brew install elixir
```

Linux:

Use your package manager to install Elixir:

```bash
Copy code
sudo apt-get update
sudo apt-get install -y elixir
```

From Source:

For the latest version, you can build Elixir from source. Instructions are available on the official website.

2. Verify Installation

After installation, open a terminal and check the Elixir version:

```bash
Copy code
```

elixir --version

3. Set Up the Interactive Elixir Shell (iex)

Elixir includes an interactive shell called iex, which allows
you to run and test code snippets quickly:

```bash
Copy code
iex
```

For example:

```elixir
Copy code
iex> IO.puts("Hello, Elixir!")
Hello, Elixir!
```

4. Install Development Tools

Mix:

Elixir includes Mix, a build tool for creating projects,
managing dependencies, and running tasks. Use it to create a
new project:

bash
Copy code

```
mix new my_project
cd my_project
mix run
```

Hex:

Hex is Elixir's package manager for managing libraries and dependencies. It comes preinstalled and can be verified by running:

bash
Copy code

```
mix hex.info
```

5. Set Up an IDE or Text Editor

Choose an editor with Elixir support, such as:

VS Code: Install the "ElixirLS" extension for syntax highlighting, debugging, and more.
IntelliJ IDEA: Use the Elixir plugin for a robust development environment.

6. Optional: Docker Setup

For isolated environments, use a Docker container:

```dockerfile
dockerfile
Copy code
FROM elixir:latest
WORKDIR /app
COPY . .
CMD ["iex"]
```

With Elixir installed and your environment set up, you are ready to explore its powerful features and start developing scalable, concurrent applications.

## 2.3 Basic Syntax and Concepts

Elixir is a dynamic, functional programming language with an expressive syntax designed for simplicity and developer productivity. Understanding its basic syntax and core concepts is essential for leveraging the language effectively.

# 1. Variables and Immutability

Variables in Elixir are immutable, meaning once assigned, their value cannot be changed. Instead, reassignment creates a new binding.

```elixir
Copy code
x = 10
IO.puts(x)  # Output: 10
x = 20
IO.puts(x)  # Output: 20 (new binding, not a modification)
```

# 2. Data Types

Elixir supports a variety of data types:

Numbers: Integers (1, 42) and floats (3.14)
Booleans: true and false
Atoms: Constants with a name, e.g., :ok, :error
Strings: Double-quoted sequences of characters, e.g., "Hello"
Lists: Ordered collections, e.g., [1, 2, 3]
Tuples: Fixed-size collections, e.g., {:ok, "Success"}

## 3. Pattern Matching

Pattern matching is a powerful feature in Elixir used for destructuring and binding values.

```elixir
Copy code
{status, message} = {:ok, "Welcome"}
IO.puts(status)   # Output: :ok
IO.puts(message)  # Output: Welcome
```

## 4. Functions

Functions are first-class citizens in Elixir. They can be defined as named or anonymous functions.

Named Functions:

Defined within a module using def.

```elixir
Copy code
defmodule Math do
  def add(a, b), do: a + b
```

end
IO.puts(Math.add(2, 3))  # Output: 5
Anonymous Functions:

Created using fn and end.

elixir
Copy code
add = fn a, b -> a + b end
IO.puts(add.(2, 3))  # Output: 5

## 5. Control Structures

Elixir provides expressive control structures for decision-making and iteration:

if and unless:

elixir
Copy code
```
if true do
  IO.puts("This is true")
end
unless false do
  IO.puts("This is also true")
```

end

case:

Pattern matches against multiple conditions.

elixir
Copy code
```elixir
case {:ok, "Hello"} do
  {:ok, message} -> IO.puts(message)  # Output: Hello
  _ -> IO.puts("No match")
end
```

cond:

Similar to if-else if chains.

elixir
Copy code
```elixir
cond do
  1 + 1 == 3 -> IO.puts("Wrong")
  1 + 1 == 2 -> IO.puts("Correct")  # Output: Correct
end
```

6. Modules

Modules group related functions and serve as a building block for applications. Defined using defmodule.

elixir
Copy code
```elixir
defmodule Greeter do
  def greet(name), do: "Hello, #{name}!"
end
IO.puts(Greeter.greet("Alice"))  # Output: Hello, Alice!
```

## 7. Pipe Operator (|>)

The pipe operator chains functions together, passing the result of one function as the input to the next.

elixir
Copy code
```elixir
"hello"
|> String.upcase()
|> IO.puts()  # Output: HELLO
```

Understanding these basics provides a solid foundation for exploring Elixir's advanced features like concurrency, fault tolerance, and metaprogramming.

# PART II: ELIXIR AND FUNCTIONAL PROGRAMMING CONCEPTS

## Chapter 3
### Immutable Data and Pure Functions

Immutable Data

In Elixir, data is immutable, meaning once a value is assigned to a variable, it cannot be altered. Instead, operations on data create new values rather than modifying the original. This ensures data consistency and eliminates side effects, making programs easier to understand and debug.

Example:

```elixir
Copy code
x = [1, 2, 3]
y = x ++ [4]  # Creates a new list
IO.inspect(x)  # Output: [1, 2, 3]
```

IO.inspect(y) # Output: [1, 2, 3, 4]

Immutability is crucial for concurrent programming, as it prevents data conflicts between processes.

Pure Functions

Pure functions are a cornerstone of functional programming. A pure function has the following characteristics:

Deterministic: It always produces the same output for the same input.
No Side Effects: It does not alter external state or interact with the outside world (e.g., no database or file modifications).

Example:

```elixir
Copy code
defmodule Math do
  def square(x), do: x * x
end
IO.puts(Math.square(4)) # Output: 16
```

Benefits of pure functions include:

Easier testing and debugging.
Enhanced predictability and reliability.
Better support for parallelism and concurrency.

By combining immutable data and pure functions, Elixir promotes robust, maintainable, and scalable applications.

3.1 Understanding Immutability

Immutability is a core concept in functional programming, and it plays a fundamental role in Elixir. It means that once a variable or data structure is created, its value cannot be changed. Instead, any operation that modifies data creates a new value, leaving the original unchanged.

Why Immutability Matters

Data Consistency

Immutability ensures that data remains stable and predictable throughout a program's execution, reducing the risk of unexpected changes.

Thread Safety

In concurrent applications, immutability prevents data conflicts between processes since no process can alter shared data.

Debugging and Maintenance

Immutable data eliminates side effects, making it easier to trace issues and reason about code.

Immutability in Practice

In Elixir, variables are bindings, not containers, meaning they cannot be modified after assignment:

```elixir
Copy code
x = 10
```

x = x + 1  # This creates a new binding, not a modification.

IO.puts(x) # Output: 11

Similarly, collections like lists or maps are immutable:

```elixir
Copy code
list = [1, 2, 3]
new_list = list ++ [4]  # Creates a new list.
IO.inspect(list)     # Output: [1, 2, 3]
IO.inspect(new_list)  # Output: [1, 2, 3, 4]
```

How Elixir Manages Immutability

Elixir relies on the BEAM virtual machine, which optimizes immutable data structures for performance. For example, instead of copying the entire structure, Elixir reuses parts of the existing data when creating new values.

Benefits of Immutability

Ease of Testing

Functions that operate on immutable data are deterministic, producing the same output for the same input, which simplifies testing.

## Concurrency

Immutable data eliminates the need for locks or synchronization in multi-process environments.

## Code Clarity

Immutability reduces unintended side effects, making code easier to read and maintain.

Immutability is not just a technical feature but a design philosophy in Elixir. It fosters safe, predictable, and scalable applications, especially in concurrent and distributed systems.

## 3.2 Writing Pure Functions in Elixir

Pure functions are a fundamental aspect of functional programming and a key feature of Elixir. A pure function is one that:

Always produces the same output for the same input (deterministic).

Has no side effects, meaning it doesn't modify external state, perform I/O operations, or interact with the outside world. Pure functions contribute to better code quality by making programs easier to test, debug, and reason about.

Characteristics of Pure Functions

Deterministic Behavior

A pure function's output depends only on its inputs, ensuring predictable results.

elixir
Copy code
```
defmodule Math do
  def square(x), do: x * x
end
IO.puts(Math.square(4)) # Output: 16
IO.puts(Math.square(4)) # Always Output: 16
```

No Side Effects

Pure functions do not modify global variables, alter data outside their scope, or produce I/O operations.

elixir
Copy code
```
def greet(name), do: "Hello, #{name}!"
IO.puts(greet("Alice"))  # Output: Hello, Alice!
```

Immutability

Pure functions operate on immutable data and return new data when necessary.

elixir
Copy code
```
def add_to_list(list, value), do: list ++ [value]
old_list = [1, 2, 3]
new_list = add_to_list(old_list, 4)
IO.inspect(old_list)  # Output: [1, 2, 3]
IO.inspect(new_list)  # Output: [1, 2, 3, 4]
```

Benefits of Pure Functions

Testability:

Since pure functions do not depend on external state, they are easy to test independently.

elixir
Copy code

```elixir
defmodule MathTest do
  use ExUnit.Case
  test "square function" do
    assert Math.square(4) == 16
  end
end
```

Concurrency:

Pure functions are inherently thread-safe, as they do not rely on shared mutable state.

Readability and Maintainability:

Pure functions simplify code by eliminating hidden dependencies and side effects.

Common Practices for Writing Pure Functions

Avoid External Dependencies:

Avoid using global variables or relying on external state. Instead, pass all required data as arguments.

Focus on Single Responsibility:

A pure function should perform one task and do it well.

elixir
Copy code
```elixir
def calculate_area(length, width), do: length * width
```

Return New Data Structures:

Always create and return new data structures instead of modifying existing ones.

elixir
Copy code
```elixir
def append_item(list, item), do: list ++ [item]
```

Pure functions form the building blocks of robust, maintainable, and scalable Elixir applications. By adhering to purity, developers can harness the full power of functional programming, ensuring predictable behavior and easier debugging.

## 3.3 Benefits of Immutability and Purity

Immutability and purity are foundational concepts in functional programming and play a crucial role in Elixir's design. Together, they promote better code quality, scalability, and maintainability. Here's how they benefit developers and applications:

1. Improved Code Predictability

Immutability ensures that data does not change unexpectedly, making the behavior of the program easier to understand.
Pure functions, which always produce the same output for the same input, eliminate uncertainty in code execution.
Example:

elixir
Copy code

```elixir
def square(x), do: x * x
IO.puts(square(5))  # Output: 25
```

## 2. Easier Testing and Debugging

Pure functions are self-contained and free of side effects, making them easy to test independently.
Debugging is simplified because immutable data eliminates issues related to unintended data mutations.

Example Test:

elixir
Copy code

```elixir
defmodule MathTest do
  use ExUnit.Case
  test "square function" do
    assert Math.square(3) == 9
  end
end
```

## 3. Enhanced Concurrency and Parallelism

Immutability prevents race conditions and data conflicts, as processes cannot modify shared data.
Pure functions are thread-safe and ideal for concurrent execution.

Example:

In Elixir, processes can work with immutable data independently without synchronization mechanisms.

elixir
Copy code
Task.async(fn -> Enum.map([1, 2, 3], &(&1 * 2)) end)

4. Reduced Side Effects

Purity ensures that functions do not alter global state, interact with external systems, or produce unintended changes.
This isolation improves program reliability and makes systems more robust.

5. Simplified Maintenance

Immutability and purity reduce hidden dependencies, making code easier to read, modify, and maintain.
Changes to one part of the codebase have minimal impact on other parts.

## 6. Better Reusability and Modularity

Pure functions can be reused in different contexts without concern for external state.
They enable modular design by breaking applications into smaller, testable components.

## 7. Facilitates Functional Programming Principles

Immutability and purity align with functional programming paradigms, such as higher-order functions and declarative coding, leading to concise and expressive code.

Example of Functional Composition:

elixir
Copy code

```
"hello"
|> String.upcase()
|> String.reverse()
# Output: "OLLEH"
```

By embracing immutability and purity, Elixir applications become more predictable, maintainable, and efficient, particularly in concurrent and distributed environments. These principles not only enhance the developer experience but also ensure the scalability and reliability of the applications.

# Chapter 4
## Higher-Order Functions and Recursion

Higher-Order Functions

A higher-order function is a function that takes one or more functions as arguments, returns a function as a result, or both. This allows for greater flexibility and abstraction in programming. In Elixir, higher-order functions enable powerful techniques like function composition and passing behavior as data.

Example:

elixir
Copy code
```
# A function that takes another function as an argument
defmodule Math do
  def apply_to_number(func, number), do: func.(number)
end
```

IO.puts(Math.apply_to_number(&(&1 * 2), 5))  # Output: 10

In this example, the apply_to_number function accepts a function (func) and a number, applying the function to the number.

Recursion

Recursion is a common technique in functional programming, where a function calls itself to solve a problem. It is often used to process data structures like lists and trees. In Elixir, recursion replaces traditional loops (e.g., for, while) found in imperative languages.

Example:

elixir
Copy code
```elixir
# Recursively summing a list of numbers
defmodule Math do
  def sum([]), do: 0
  def sum([head | tail]), do: head + sum(tail)
end

IO.puts(Math.sum([1, 2, 3, 4]))  # Output: 10
```

In this example, the sum function calls itself until it reaches an empty list ([]), at which point it returns 0.

Both higher-order functions and recursion are powerful tools in Elixir, enabling elegant and concise solutions to complex problems. They allow developers to write more modular, reusable, and expressive code while adhering to functional programming principles.

## 4.1 Understanding Higher-Order Functions

In functional programming, higher-order functions are a powerful and essential concept. A higher-order function is a function that:

Takes one or more functions as arguments,
Returns a function as a result, or both.

This ability to treat functions as first-class citizens—meaning they can be passed around and returned like any other data type—enables more abstract and flexible programming.

Why Higher-Order Functions Matter

Higher-order functions allow for:

Abstraction: By passing functions as arguments, you can abstract common patterns and behaviors, leading to more modular and reusable code.
Composability: You can create more complex behavior by combining smaller, simpler functions, often leading to cleaner and more readable code.
Functional Composition: Functions can be composed together to create new functionality without explicitly needing to define all the steps.

Examples of Higher-Order Functions in Elixir

Passing Functions as Arguments

Elixir allows you to pass functions as arguments to other functions. This can be useful for operations like transformations, mapping, and filtering.

Example:

```elixir
Copy code
defmodule Math do
  def apply(func, value), do: func.(value)
end

IO.puts(Math.apply(&(&1 * 2), 5)) # Output: 10
```

Returning Functions from Other Functions

A higher-order function can return another function. This is useful for creating custom behavior dynamically.
Example:

```elixir
Copy code
defmodule Math do
  def multiplier(factor) do
    fn x -> x * factor end
```

```
  end
end
```

```
multiply_by_3 = Math.multiplier(3)
IO.puts(multiply_by_3.(4))  # Output: 12
```

Common Use Cases for Higher-Order Functions

Map, Filter, and Reduce
Functions like Enum.map, Enum.filter, and Enum.reduce
are higher-order functions because they take a function as an
argument to apply to each element of a list.

Example:

elixir
Copy code
```
IO.inspect(Enum.map([1, 2, 3], &(&1 * 2)))  # Output: [2,
4, 6]
```

Currying
Higher-order functions can be used to implement currying,
where you break down a function that takes multiple

arguments into a series of functions that each take one argument.

Example:

```elixir
Copy code
defmodule Math do
  def add(a), do: fn b -> a + b end
end

add_2 = Math.add(2)
IO.puts(add_2.(3)) # Output: 5
```

Benefits of Higher-Order Functions

Modularity: Higher-order functions promote code reuse by allowing you to define general operations that can be customized with specific behaviors.

Flexibility: They allow dynamic creation and modification of behaviors by passing and returning functions.

Composability: You can compose functions together, making your code more expressive and concise.

Conclusion

Higher-order functions are a central concept in Elixir and functional programming in general. They allow developers to write more abstract, flexible, and reusable code, ultimately leading to cleaner and more maintainable applications. By understanding and utilizing higher-order functions, developers can take full advantage of Elixir's functional programming capabilities.

## 4.2 Exploring Recursion in Elixir

Recursion is a key concept in functional programming, where a function calls itself to solve smaller instances of a problem. In Elixir, recursion is commonly used in place of loops for processing collections and handling iterative tasks. Since Elixir does not have traditional looping constructs like for or while, recursion is an essential tool for repeating computations.

How Recursion Works in Elixir

A recursive function typically has two parts:

Base Case: The simplest instance of the problem, where recursion stops.

Recursive Case: The part of the function that calls itself with a smaller or simpler problem.

Elixir uses pattern matching to determine which part of the recursion to execute, allowing elegant and efficient solutions.

Basic Example of Recursion

To demonstrate how recursion works, let's start with a simple example: calculating the sum of a list of numbers.

```elixir
Copy code
defmodule Math do
  def sum([]), do: 0  # Base case: an empty list returns 0
  def sum([head | tail]), do: head + sum(tail)  # Recursive case
end

IO.puts(Math.sum([1, 2, 3, 4]))  # Output: 10
```

In this example:

The base case is when the list is empty ([]), in which case the function returns 0.

The recursive case processes the list by extracting the first element (head) and calling the sum function on the remaining list (tail).

Understanding Recursion with Pattern Matching

Pattern matching in Elixir makes recursion intuitive and concise. You can define different behavior for different kinds of input (e.g., an empty list or a non-empty list). This allows for clear and concise recursive functions.

For example, in the following function, the first clause matches an empty list, and the second clause matches a non-empty list:

```elixir
Copy code
defmodule Math do
  def factorial(0), do: 1  # Base case
  def factorial(n), do: n * factorial(n - 1)  # Recursive case
end
```

```
IO.puts(Math.factorial(5))  # Output: 120
```

The function factorial/1 calls itself with a smaller value of n, ultimately reaching the base case where n equals 0.

Tail Recursion

Tail recursion is a specific form of recursion where the recursive call is the last operation performed in the function. Tail-recursive functions are optimized by the compiler to reuse the current function's stack frame, preventing stack overflow errors and improving performance.

To make the previous sum/1 function tail-recursive, we introduce an accumulator:

```elixir
Copy code
defmodule Math do
   def sum(list), do: sum(list, 0)   # Initial call with an accumulator
   def sum([], acc), do: acc   # Base case: return the accumulator
```

```
def sum([head | tail], acc), do: sum(tail, acc + head)  #
Recursive case
end

IO.puts(Math.sum([1, 2, 3, 4])) # Output: 10
```

Here, the accumulator (acc) keeps track of the running total, and the function's recursive call is the last action, ensuring tail recursion.

Benefits of Recursion in Elixir

Expressiveness: Recursion allows complex iterative processes to be expressed clearly and declaratively.
Functional Style: It aligns with the functional programming paradigm, where immutability and avoiding side effects are emphasized.
Scalability: Tail-recursive functions are highly efficient and can handle large datasets without the risk of stack overflow errors.

When to Use Recursion

Recursion is especially useful when:

The problem involves processing lists, trees, or other recursive data structures.

You need to break a problem into smaller subproblems.

You want to avoid mutable state and embrace functional programming principles.


Conclusion

Recursion is a vital concept in Elixir, allowing developers to handle repetitive tasks and process data in a functional and declarative manner. By using recursion, you can avoid mutable state and take full advantage of Elixir's immutable data structures, leading to more robust and scalable applications. With Elixir's powerful pattern matching and tail recursion optimization, recursive functions can be both elegant and efficient.


4.3 Common Patterns in Recursion

Recursion is a versatile tool in functional programming, and it often follows certain patterns that make it easier to implement and understand. In Elixir, recursion is widely used to solve problems that require iterative processing, such as traversing lists, calculating values, or performing operations on trees and other data structures. Here are some of the most common recursion patterns you'll encounter:

1. Linear Recursion

Linear recursion is the simplest and most straightforward pattern, where each recursive call processes one element of the data structure before making the next recursive call. It's commonly used for tasks like summing numbers or checking conditions in a list.

Example:

```elixir
Copy code
defmodule Math do
  def length([]), do: 0  # Base case: empty list has length 0
  def length([_head | tail]), do: 1 + length(tail)  # Recursive case: 1 + length of tail
end

IO.puts(Math.length([1, 2, 3, 4]))  # Output: 4
```

Here, the length/1 function counts the elements of a list by recursively calling itself on the tail of the list and adding 1 for each element.

2. Tail Recursion

Tail recursion is a special form of recursion where the recursive call is the last action performed in the function. This pattern is crucial for efficiency, as Elixir optimizes tail-recursive functions to avoid growing the call stack, thus preventing stack overflow errors.

Example:

```elixir
Copy code
defmodule Math do
  def factorial(n), do: factorial(n, 1)  # Initial call with an accumulator
  def factorial(0, acc), do: acc  # Base case: return the accumulator
  def factorial(n, acc), do: factorial(n - 1, acc * n) # Recursive case
end
```

```elixir
IO.puts(Math.factorial(5)) # Output: 120
```

In this example, the accumulator (acc) carries the result, and the recursive call is the last operation. This ensures that the function runs in constant stack space, making it more efficient for large numbers.

3. Accumulating Recursion

Accumulating recursion is similar to tail recursion but focuses on collecting or accumulating results as you process elements. Instead of returning a simple value, you build up a result through each recursive call. This pattern is often used in situations where you need to compute an aggregate result, like a sum, product, or concatenated string.

Example:

```elixir
Copy code
defmodule Math do
    def sum([], acc), do: acc   # Base case: return the accumulator
```

```elixir
  def sum([head | tail], acc), do: sum(tail, acc + head)  #
Recursive case
end

IO.puts(Math.sum([1, 2, 3, 4], 0))  # Output: 10
```

In this example, the function sum/2 accumulates the sum of
the list in the accumulator (acc). Each recursive call adds the
current element to the accumulator, and the base case
returns the accumulated result.

4. Divide and Conquer

The divide-and-conquer recursion pattern involves breaking
a problem into smaller subproblems, solving each
subproblem recursively, and then combining the results.
This is particularly useful for sorting algorithms (like merge
sort) or searching through large datasets (like binary search).

Example (Binary Search):

```elixir
Copy code
defmodule Search do
```

```
def binary_search([], _target), do: :not_found # Base case:
empty list
def binary_search([mid | rest], target) when mid == target,
do: :found # Found target
def binary_search([mid | rest], target) when target < mid,
do: binary_search(Enum.take(rest, div(length(rest), 2)),
target) # Search left half
def binary_search([mid | rest], target), do:
binary_search(Enum.drop(rest, div(length(rest), 2)), target)
# Search right half
end

IO.puts(Search.binary_search([1, 2, 3, 4, 5], 3)) # Output:
:found
```

In the binary search example, the list is divided in half each time, with the target being searched in either the left or right half depending on its value relative to the middle element.

5. Multiple Recursions (Tree Recursion)

Tree recursion occurs when a function calls itself more than once during its execution. This pattern is often seen when working with tree-like structures, where each node may have multiple children, leading to recursive calls on multiple branches.

Example (Factorial Tree Recursion):

elixir
Copy code
```
defmodule Math do
  def factorial(0), do: 1  # Base case
  def factorial(n), do: n * factorial(n - 1)  # Recursive case
end
```

IO.puts(Math.factorial(4))  # Output: 24

Each time the function calls itself on n - 1, it is essentially branching out to compute the factorial of smaller numbers, leading to a "tree" of recursive calls.

6. Mutual Recursion

Mutual recursion occurs when two or more functions call each other in a cycle. This can be helpful for problems that require multiple steps to complete and can be broken down into multiple related functions.

Example:

```elixir
defmodule Parity do
  def even?(0), do: true
  def even?(n), do: odd?(n - 1)

  def odd?(0), do: false
  def odd?(n), do: even?(n - 1)
end

IO.puts(Parity.even?(4))  # Output: true
```

In this example, the even?/1 and odd?/1 functions call each other recursively to check whether a number is even or odd, depending on the value of n.

Conclusion

Recursion is a powerful tool in Elixir that allows you to solve complex problems with clean and concise code. The common patterns in recursion, such as linear recursion, tail recursion, accumulating recursion, divide-and-conquer, tree recursion, and mutual recursion, provide versatile approaches for tackling a wide range of problems. Understanding these patterns allows you to choose the right recursion strategy based on the problem's requirements, ultimately leading to more efficient and maintainable solutions.

# Chapter 5
## Pattern Matching and Guards

Pattern Matching in Elixir is a powerful mechanism that allows you to check and deconstruct data structures (such as tuples, lists, or maps) in a concise and expressive way. It enables you to write concise and readable code by matching the shape of data with predefined patterns.

Guards extend pattern matching by allowing you to specify conditions that can be used to determine whether a function should be executed. Guards are used in functions to restrict which values can be matched, enabling more controlled and safe execution of code.

Pattern Matching Examples:

Matching on lists:

```elixir
Copy code
defmodule Example do
```

```elixir
  def sum([]), do: 0  # Base case: empty list returns 0
    def sum([head | tail]), do: head + sum(tail)  # Recursive
case
end
```

Matching on tuples:

elixir
Copy code
```elixir
defmodule Example do
  def greeting({:hello, name}), do: "Hello, #{name}!"
  def greeting(_), do: "Unknown greeting"
end
```

Guards Examples:

Using guards to check conditions:

elixir
Copy code
```elixir
defmodule Example do
  def is_even?(n) when rem(n, 2) == 0, do: true
  def is_even?(_), do: false
end
```

Guard clauses for ranges:

elixir
Copy code

```elixir
defmodule Example do
  def categorize_age(age) when age < 18, do: "Minor"
  def categorize_age(age) when age >= 18 and age < 65, do:
"Adult"
  def categorize_age(_), do: "Senior"
end
```

In summary, pattern matching and guards provide powerful tools for handling various data scenarios in Elixir, making code concise, readable, and safe by reducing the need for conditional statements.

## 5.1 Basics of Pattern Matching

Pattern matching is a fundamental feature of Elixir that allows you to destructure and extract values from data structures in a simple and expressive way. Unlike traditional variable assignments in other languages, pattern matching works by comparing the structure of the data on both sides of the match operator (=). If the structures match, variables are bound to values; otherwise, an error is raised.

The Match Operator (=)

The = operator in Elixir is not an assignment operator but a match operator. It attempts to match the pattern on the left-hand side with the value on the right-hand side.

Examples:

elixir
Copy code
```
x = 10      # Matches and binds x to 10
{a, b} = {1, 2} # Matches and binds a = 1, b = 2
[head | tail] = [1, 2, 3] # Matches head = 1, tail = [2, 3]
```
If the structures don't match, Elixir raises a

MatchError:

elixir
Copy code
```
{a, b} = {1, 2, 3} # Error: unmatched data
```

Deconstructing Data Structures

Pattern matching works seamlessly with Elixir's built-in data types like lists, tuples, and maps:

Tuples:

elixir
Copy code
```
{name, age} = {"Alice", 30}
IO.puts(name)  # Output: Alice
IO.puts(age)   # Output: 30
```

Lists:

elixir
Copy code
```
[head | tail] = [10, 20, 30]
IO.puts(head)  # Output: 10
IO.inspect(tail)  # Output: [20, 30]
```
Maps:

elixir
Copy code
```
%{key: value} = %{key: "value"}
IO.puts(value)  # Output: value
```

Using the Pin Operator (^)

The pin operator (^) prevents reassignment of variables during pattern matching. It allows matching against the current value of a variable instead of rebinding it.

Example:

```elixir
Copy code
x = 42
^x = 42  # Match succeeds
^x = 43  # Error: no match since x is not 43
```

Pattern Matching in Function Definitions

Elixir leverages pattern matching in function definitions to enable multiple function clauses, simplifying conditional logic.

Example:

```elixir
Copy code
```

```
defmodule Example do
  def greet({:ok, name}), do: "Hello, #{name}!"
  def greet({:error, _reason}), do: "Something went wrong."
end
```

```
IO.puts(Example.greet({:ok, "Alice"}))   # Output: Hello,
Alice!
```

Benefits of Pattern Matching

Clarity and Readability: Simplifies extracting values from complex structures.

Error Prevention: Fails early when the data structure doesn't match the expected pattern.

Declarative Code: Reduces reliance on imperative constructs like if or switch.
Robust Function Definitions: Allows writing concise, condition-specific function clauses.

Conclusion

Pattern matching is a core feature that enhances Elixir's functional programming paradigm. It enables developers to write expressive, error-resistant code while providing a natural way to destructure and process data. Mastering pattern matching is crucial for leveraging the full power of Elixir.

5.2 Using Guards for More Robust Functions

Guards in Elixir are a powerful way to refine pattern matching by adding conditional logic to function clauses. They allow you to enforce additional constraints on the data being matched, making your functions more precise, expressive, and robust. Guards are used in conjunction with the when keyword and can include a variety of built-in functions and operators.

Why Use Guards?

Enhanced Clarity: They clarify the intent of function clauses by specifying additional conditions.
Error Prevention: Help prevent invalid or unexpected inputs from being processed.

Improved Functionality: Allow for more specific matching criteria without cluttering code with nested conditionals.

Syntax of Guards

Guards are written after a pattern match using the when keyword.

Example:

```elixir
Copy code
defmodule Example do
  def categorize_age(age) when age < 18, do: "Minor"
  def categorize_age(age) when age >= 18 and age < 65, do: "Adult"
  def categorize_age(age) when age >= 65, do: "Senior"
end

IO.puts(Example.categorize_age(25)) # Output: Adult
```

Commonly Used Guard Expressions

Type Checking:

is_integer/1

is_float/1

is_binary/1

is_map/1

elixir

Copy code

```
defmodule TypeCheck do
  def print_type(value) when is_integer(value), do: "Integer"
  def print_type(value) when is_binary(value), do: "String"
end
```

```
IO.puts(TypeCheck.print_type(42)) # Output: Integer
```

Comparison Operators:

<, <=, >, >=

elixir

Copy code

```
defmodule Compare do
  def check_value(x) when x > 10, do: "Greater than 10"
  def check_value(x) when x <= 10, do: "10 or less"
end
```

```
IO.puts(Compare.check_value(15))    # Output: Greater
than 10
```

Boolean Logic:

and, or, not
elixir
Copy code
```
defmodule BooleanLogic do
  def categorize(x) when x > 0 and rem(x, 2) == 0, do:
"Positive Even"
  def categorize(x) when x > 0 and rem(x, 2) != 0, do:
"Positive Odd"
end
```

Arithmetic:

rem/2 (remainder)
div/2 (integer division)
elixir
Copy code
```
defmodule Arithmetic do
  def even_or_odd(x) when rem(x, 2) == 0, do: "Even"
  def even_or_odd(_x), do: "Odd"
end
```

Combining Pattern Matching and Guards

Pattern matching and guards work together to make function definitions concise and robust.

Example: Handling Lists:

elixir
Copy code
```elixir
defmodule ListHandler do
  def process_list([head | tail]) when is_integer(head), do: "Starts with an integer"
  def process_list([head | tail]) when is_binary(head), do: "Starts with a string"
  def process_list([]), do: "Empty list"
end


IO.puts(ListHandler.process_list([1, 2, 3]))   # Output: Starts with an integer
IO.puts(ListHandler.process_list(["hello", "world"]))   # Output: Starts with a string
```

Caveats and Limitations

Guards only allow a subset of Elixir's expressions for safety reasons (e.g., no function calls other than allowed guard functions).

Guards cannot use user-defined functions or perform complex logic.

Conclusion

Guards add an extra layer of precision and safety to Elixir functions. By combining guards with pattern matching, developers can create highly robust and maintainable code. Mastering guards is essential for writing clear, concise, and expressive Elixir applications.

5.3 Practical Use Cases

Elixir's functional programming model, enriched by pattern matching, immutability, and guards, provides robust tools for real-world applications. These features allow developers to write expressive, efficient, and maintainable code that solves complex problems. Below are some practical use cases demonstrating the power and flexibility of Elixir.

1. Web Development with Phoenix Framework

Elixir is widely used in building scalable web applications through the Phoenix framework, which leverages Elixir's concurrency and fault-tolerance capabilities.

Use Case: Building real-time applications like chat platforms or dashboards.
Features Used: Pattern matching for routing, immutable state for managing requests, and functional pipelines for cleaner code.

Example:

```elixir
Copy code
defmodule MyAppWeb.Router do
  use Phoenix.Router

  pipeline :browser do
    plug :accepts, ["html"]
    plug :fetch_session
  end
```

```elixir
  scope "/", MyAppWeb do
    get "/", PageController, :index
  end
end
```

2. Concurrent Data Processing

Elixir's lightweight processes make it ideal for handling concurrent tasks, such as processing large datasets or streaming data in parallel.

Use Case: Real-time log aggregation and monitoring.

Features Used: Processes, Tasks, and Supervisors for fault tolerance and scalability.
Example:

```elixir
Copy code
defmodule LogProcessor do
  def start_processing(logs) do
        Enum.each(logs, fn log -> Task.start(fn ->
process_log(log) end) end)
  end
```

```elixir
  defp process_log(log), do: IO.puts("Processing: #{log}")
end
```

3. Building APIs

With Elixir, you can create fast and resilient APIs for handling high traffic while maintaining data integrity.

Use Case: RESTful or GraphQL API development.

Features Used: Functional design for request handling and Plug library for middleware.
Example:

```elixir
elixir
Copy code
defmodule MyAPI do
  use Plug.Router

  plug :match
  plug :dispatch

  get "/hello" do
    send_resp(conn, 200, "Hello, world!")
  end
```

end

## 4. Real-Time Systems

Elixir excels in building systems requiring real-time capabilities, such as IoT applications or collaborative platforms.

Use Case: Multi-user collaborative tools like document editors or game servers.
Features Used: PubSub for real-time message broadcasting and pattern matching for routing events.

Example:

```elixir
Copy code
defmodule ChatRoom do
  def broadcast_message(room, message) do
        Phoenix.PubSub.broadcast(MyApp.PubSub, room, {:new_message, message})
  end
end
```

## 5. Data Transformation and ETL Pipelines

Elixir's functional paradigm and immutability make it an excellent choice for data transformation tasks.

Use Case: Processing and normalizing large datasets.
Features Used: Functional pipelines, pattern matching, and higher-order functions.

Example:

```elixir
Copy code
defmodule DataTransformer do
  def process(data) do
    data
    |> Enum.map(&normalize/1)
    |> Enum.filter(&valid?/1)
  end

  defp normalize(record), do: Map.update(record, :value, 0, &(&1 * 2))
  defp valid?(record), do: record[:value] > 0
end
```

6. Fault-Tolerant Applications

Elixir's robust supervision tree ensures that systems recover automatically from failures.

Use Case: Payment processing systems or message queues.

Features Used: Supervisors and OTP behavior for reliability.

Example:

```elixir
Copy code
defmodule MyApp.Supervisor do
  use Supervisor

  def start_link do
    Supervisor.start_link(__MODULE__, [])
  end

  def init(_) do
    children = [
      {Task, fn -> perform_task() end}
    ]

    Supervisor.init(children, strategy: :one_for_one)
```

end
end

## 7. Chatbots and Natural Language Processing

Elixir is also used for building chatbots and conversational interfaces, leveraging libraries like ExGram or connecting to NLP services.

Use Case: Customer service bots or AI-driven assistants.

Features Used: Pattern matching for interpreting commands and integrating external APIs.
Example:

elixir
Copy code
```elixir
defmodule ChatBot do
  def respond("hello"), do: "Hi there!"
  def respond("bye"), do: "Goodbye!"
  def respond(_), do: "I don't understand that command."
end
```

Conclusion

Elixir's features make it suitable for a wide range of practical use cases, from web development to real-time systems and fault-tolerant applications. By leveraging its functional and concurrent capabilities, developers can build systems that are not only powerful and efficient but also maintainable and reliable.

# PART III: CONCURRENCY AND SCALABILITY WITH ELIXIR

## Chapter 6
## Processes in Elixir

Elixir's processes are lightweight, isolated, and highly efficient units of computation, designed to handle concurrency and parallelism seamlessly. Unlike operating system processes, Elixir processes are managed by the BEAM VM (Erlang's virtual machine), enabling the creation of thousands or even millions of concurrent processes without significant overhead.

Key Features of Elixir Processes

Isolation: Processes do not share memory, ensuring fault tolerance and data integrity.

Lightweight: They consume minimal system resources, making them ideal for highly concurrent applications.

Concurrency: Elixir processes run concurrently, leveraging multicore processors effectively.

Fault Tolerance: Crashed processes can be restarted by supervisors without affecting the entire system.

Creating Processes

spawn/1 Function: Starts a new process.

```elixir
Copy code
spawn(fn -> IO.puts("Hello from a process!") end)
```

send/2 and receive: Enable message passing between processes.

```elixir
Copy code
spawn(fn ->
  receive do
    {:hello, msg} -> IO.puts("Message received: #{msg}")
  end
end)
```

```elixir
send(self(), {:hello, "Hi there!"})
```

Tasks: Simplified abstractions for processes.

elixir
Copy code
```elixir
Task.start(fn -> IO.puts("Task executed!") end)
```

Use Cases

Concurrent Data Processing: Processing multiple streams of data simultaneously.

Real-Time Systems: Handling user interactions or IoT device communication.
Supervised Applications: Creating robust systems where processes are monitored and restarted on failure.

Conclusion

Processes are foundational to Elixir's concurrency model, enabling developers to build scalable, resilient, and fault-tolerant applications. By mastering processes, you can unlock the full potential of Elixir's capabilities.

## 6.1 The Actor Model and Processes

The Actor Model is a conceptual model for handling concurrency, and Elixir embraces it through its lightweight, isolated processes. This model is central to how Elixir processes communicate and manage concurrency efficiently.

What is the Actor Model?

The Actor Model is a computational model where actors are the fundamental units of computation. Each actor is an independent process that:

Encapsulates state: Each actor has its own private state.

Receives messages: Actors communicate by receiving messages, which may contain data.
Performs actions: Upon receiving a message, an actor can perform a computation, modify its internal state, and send messages to other actors.

How Elixir Implements the Actor Model

In Elixir, processes are the embodiment of actors. Each process in Elixir can:

Send messages to other processes using send/2.
Receive messages through the receive block.
Perform actions based on the received messages.

Since each process is isolated, it does not share memory, ensuring that no process can directly modify the state of another. This eliminates concerns about race conditions, making Elixir highly suitable for concurrent and parallel programming.

Key Concepts of Processes in Elixir

Isolation: Every process in Elixir runs independently with its own state. They do not share memory, which reduces the complexity of managing concurrent processes.

Message Passing: Processes communicate exclusively through asynchronous message passing. When a process wants to send a message to another process, it uses the send/2 function. The receiving process handles the message using the receive block.

```elixir
Copy code
defmodule Example do
 def send_message do
  self() |> send({:hello, "World"})
 end

 def receive_message do
  receive do
   {:hello, msg} -> IO.puts("Received: #{msg}")
  end
 end
end
```

Concurrency: Elixir processes run concurrently on the BEAM VM, which schedules them efficiently across multiple cores, enabling parallel execution.

Fault Tolerance: If an actor (process) fails, it does not affect others. Elixir leverages the Supervisor model to monitor processes and restart them if needed, ensuring fault tolerance and system reliability.

Benefits of the Actor Model in Elixir

Concurrency Made Easy: Elixir's actor model abstracts away the complexity of managing threads, locks, and memory access. It allows developers to focus on the logic rather than low-level concurrency issues.

Scalability: Elixir's lightweight processes allow the system to scale effortlessly. It can handle millions of processes concurrently with little resource overhead.

Fault Tolerance: In case a process crashes, its state is not shared with others, and it can be restarted by a supervisor without affecting the rest of the system, improving reliability.

Simplified Communication: Since processes communicate through messages, code becomes cleaner, as there are no shared mutable states to synchronize or protect.

Example: A Simple Actor System
elixir
Copy code

```elixir
defmodule Counter do
  def start do
    spawn(fn -> loop(0) end)
```

```
    end

  defp loop(count) do
    receive do
      :increment ->
        IO.puts("Count: #{count + 1}")
        loop(count + 1)
      :decrement ->
        IO.puts("Count: #{count - 1}")
        loop(count - 1)
      :get_count ->
        IO.puts("Current Count: #{count}")
        loop(count)
    end
  end
end
```

In the above example, the Counter module represents a simple actor that maintains its own state (count). It can receive messages to increment, decrement, or fetch its current state, and each message is processed independently.

Real-World Applications

Real-Time Applications: Elixir's actor model is well-suited for real-time systems such as messaging platforms, notifications, and live data streams where concurrency and fault tolerance are critical.

Distributed Systems: The actor model allows Elixir processes to be distributed across multiple machines seamlessly. Processes can send messages to each other, even if they are running on different nodes in a distributed Elixir system.

Microservices Architecture: Elixir processes can serve as microservices that communicate via messages, making it easier to develop and maintain distributed services that are loosely coupled but highly responsive.

Conclusion

The Actor Model provides a robust way to handle concurrency by treating each process as an independent actor that communicates asynchronously through messages. In Elixir, processes are the core abstraction, allowing developers to build scalable, concurrent, and fault-tolerant applications. By embracing the Actor Model, Elixir enables highly efficient systems that are well-suited for real-time, distributed, and large-scale applications.

## 6.2 Spawning and Managing Processes

Elixir's lightweight processes are a cornerstone of its concurrency model, allowing developers to build scalable and fault-tolerant applications. Processes in Elixir are not tied to operating system threads but are managed by the BEAM VM, enabling efficient execution and management of thousands or even millions of processes simultaneously.

Spawning Processes

The spawn/1 and spawn/3 functions are used to create new processes in Elixir.

Using spawn/1: This function starts a process that executes the provided anonymous function.

elixir
Copy code

```
spawn(fn -> IO.puts("Hello from a new process!") end)
```

Output:

```
arduino
Copy code
Hello from a new process!
```

Using spawn/3: This function starts a process to run a specific function from a module.

```
elixir
Copy code
defmodule Example do
  def greet do
    IO.puts("Hello from Example module!")
  end
end
```

```
spawn(Example, :greet, [])
```

Output:

```
javascript
Copy code
```

Hello from Example module!

Managing Processes

Process Identifiers (PIDs): Every process has a unique identifier (PID). You can use the self/0 function to retrieve the PID of the current process.

elixir
Copy code
```
IO.puts("Current PID: #{inspect(self())}")
```
Sending Messages: Use send/2 to send messages to a process.

elixir
Copy code
```
pid = spawn(fn ->
  receive do
   {:hello, msg} -> IO.puts("Message received: #{msg}")
  end
end)

send(pid, {:hello, "Hi there!"})
```
Output:

mathematica

Copy code

Message received: Hi there!

Receiving Messages: Use the receive block to handle messages sent to a process.

elixir
Copy code
```elixir
receive do
  {:hello, msg} -> IO.puts("Received: #{msg}")
  :stop -> IO.puts("Stopping process")
after
  5000 -> IO.puts("No messages received")
end
```

Linking Processes: Use spawn_link/1 or spawn_link/3 to create linked processes. If one process crashes, the linked process will also terminate, making it useful for error propagation.

elixir
Copy code
```elixir
spawn_link(fn -> raise "This process will crash" end)
```

Monitoring Processes: Use spawn_monitor/1 or spawn_monitor/3 to monitor a process. If the monitored process crashes, the monitoring process receives a message.

elixir
Copy code
```
{pid, ref} = spawn_monitor(fn -> raise "Crash this process" end)
```

```
receive do
  {:DOWN, ^ref, :process, ^pid, reason} ->
    IO.puts("Process #{inspect(pid)} crashed with reason: #{inspect(reason)}")
end
```

Best Practices for Managing Processes

Supervisors: Use supervisors to manage process lifecycles and automatically restart crashed processes.

elixir
Copy code
```
defmodule MyApp.Supervisor do
  use Supervisor
```

```elixir
def start_link(_) do
  Supervisor.start_link(__MODULE__, [])
end

def init(_) do
  children = [
    {Task, fn -> IO.puts("Task running!") end}
  ]

  Supervisor.init(children, strategy: :one_for_one)
  end
end
```

Avoid Overhead: Use Elixir processes for isolated tasks but avoid over-creating processes for trivial computations.

Graceful Shutdown: Ensure processes handle shutdown messages to clean up resources before terminating.

```elixir
Copy code
defmodule GracefulProcess do
  def start do
    spawn(fn -> loop() end)
  end
```

```
defp loop do
  receive do
   :stop -> IO.puts("Stopping process gracefully")
   msg ->
    IO.puts("Received: #{inspect(msg)}")
    loop()
  end
 end
end
```

## Conclusion

Spawning and managing processes in Elixir is straightforward and efficient, thanks to the BEAM VM's concurrency model. By using tools like spawn, message passing, process linking, and monitoring, developers can create resilient and scalable systems. Combined with supervision trees, Elixir processes form the foundation for building fault-tolerant and high-performance applications.

## 6.3 Messaging Between Processes

Messaging between processes in Elixir is the foundation of its concurrency model. Processes in Elixir are isolated, meaning they do not share memory. Instead, they communicate via asynchronous message passing, which ensures thread safety and avoids race conditions.

Key Features of Messaging in Elixir

Asynchronous Communication: Messages are sent to a process's mailbox and processed when the process retrieves them.

Immutable Messages: Messages are copied between processes, ensuring data integrity.

No Shared State: Processes do not directly access each other's state, promoting fault tolerance and scalability.

Sending Messages

Messages are sent using the send/2 function, where the first argument is the process identifier (PID) and the second is the message.

elixir

```
Copy code
pid = spawn(fn ->
  receive do
    {:hello, msg} -> IO.puts("Message received: #{msg}")
  end
end)

send(pid, {:hello, "Hello, Process!"})
Output:
```

arduino
```
Copy code
Message received: Hello, Process!
```

Receiving Messages

Messages sent to a process are stored in its mailbox. The receive block retrieves and handles these messages:

elixir
```
Copy code
receive do
  {:greet, name} -> IO.puts("Hello, #{name}!")
  :stop -> IO.puts("Stopping process")
after
```

```
  5000 -> IO.puts("No messages received within 5 seconds")
end
```

Pattern Matching: Elixir uses pattern matching to select messages from the mailbox.

Timeouts: The after clause handles cases where no message is received within a specified time.

Bidirectional Communication

Processes can exchange messages for two-way communication:

```elixir
Copy code
parent = self()

spawn(fn ->
  send(parent, {:response, "Message received"})
end)

receive do
  {:response, msg} -> IO.puts("Received: #{msg}")
end
```

Output:

makefile
Copy code
Received: Message received

Process Identification

To send a message, you need the PID of the target process. Use self/0 to get the PID of the current process or store PIDs when spawning processes.

elixir
Copy code
pid = spawn(fn -> IO.puts("Process started with PID: #{inspect(self())}") end)

Messaging Use Cases

Work Delegation: Distribute tasks among multiple worker processes.
Inter-Process Communication: Share results or signals between processes.
Coordination: Coordinate state or events in real-time applications.

Supervision and Fault Tolerance

Messaging is also integral to Elixir's supervision model. Supervisors monitor processes and restart them upon failure. Communication ensures error signals and updates are properly handled.

Best Practices

Avoid Mailbox Overflow: Ensure processes handle messages quickly to prevent mailbox buildup.
Use Pattern Matching Carefully: Define clear patterns for message handling to avoid missing important messages.
Graceful Shutdowns: Design processes to recognize and handle shutdown signals (e.g., :stop).
Monitor Long-Running Processes: Use spawn_monitor/1 or spawn_link/1 to keep track of process states.

Conclusion

Messaging between processes in Elixir enables safe, asynchronous communication, laying the groundwork for building concurrent and fault-tolerant applications. By leveraging tools like send/2 and receive, developers can design systems that are both scalable and resilient.

# Chapter 7 .
## Supervisors and Fault Tolerance

Supervisors are a core feature of Elixir's fault-tolerant design. They manage the lifecycle of processes, automatically restarting them when they crash. This supervision strategy is crucial for building resilient, self-healing systems.

What Are Supervisors?

A supervisor is a process that monitors other processes, called child processes, and ensures they are always running. If a child process fails, the supervisor restarts it according to a specified strategy.

Supervision Strategies

One-for-One: Restarts only the crashed child process.
One-for-All: Restarts all child processes if one crashes.
Rest-for-One: Restarts the crashed process and all processes started after it.
Simple-One-for-One: Designed for dynamically added child processes, restarting only the specific crashed one.

## Defining a Supervisor

Supervisors are defined using the Supervisor module.

```elixir
Copy code
defmodule MyApp.Supervisor do
  use Supervisor

  def start_link(_) do
    Supervisor.start_link(__MODULE__, [])
  end

  def init(_) do
    children = [
      {Task, fn -> IO.puts("Task running!") end}
    ]

    Supervisor.init(children, strategy: :one_for_one)
  end
end
```

## Fault Tolerance Benefits

Crash Isolation: Crashes are contained to individual processes, preventing system-wide failures.

Self-Healing: Supervisors automatically restart failed processes.

Error Propagation: Linked processes ensure errors are properly communicated and managed.

Best Practices

Use Supervision Trees: Nest supervisors for modular fault-tolerance.

Monitor resource usage to avoid cascading failures.

Define clear restart strategies for specific application needs.

Supervisors are vital for maintaining uptime and reliability, enabling developers to build robust, concurrent applications with minimal manual intervention.

7.1 The Role of Supervisors in Elixir Applications

In Elixir, supervisors are fundamental to building robust, fault-tolerant systems. They play a critical role in ensuring that the application continues to function smoothly, even in the face of process failures. By automatically managing the lifecycle of child processes, supervisors help to create self-healing applications that can recover from errors without manual intervention.

What Do Supervisors Do?

A supervisor is a process responsible for starting, monitoring, and restarting other processes, known as child processes, when they fail. Supervisors define how their child processes should be restarted in the event of a failure, which is key to the fault-tolerant nature of Elixir applications.

The key responsibilities of supervisors include:

Starting Child Processes: Supervisors manage the initiation of child processes, ensuring they are started as per the defined strategy.
Monitoring Child Processes: They track the health and status of child processes.

Restarting Crashed Processes: If a child process crashes or fails, the supervisor ensures it is restarted based on the specified strategy.

Supervision Strategies

Supervisors in Elixir can be configured with different restart strategies to manage failures in various ways:

One-for-One: Only the crashed process is restarted. This is the most commonly used strategy, where the failure of one child process does not affect the others.

Example: A web request handler crashing does not affect the database connection pool.

One-for-All: If one child process crashes, all child processes are restarted. This is useful when the child processes are tightly coupled.

Example: A set of processes that all rely on the same state and need to be reset together.

Rest-for-One: If a child process crashes, it and all the child processes started after it are restarted. This strategy is ideal when processes are dependent on one another.

Example: A sequence of tasks where one task failure might affect all subsequent tasks.

Simple-One-for-One: This is a variant used when the children are dynamically added, typically for scenarios where many similar processes need to be spawned, like workers handling tasks in parallel.

Example: A pool of workers to handle incoming requests.

Defining a Supervisor in Elixir

Supervisors are defined using the Supervisor module. Here's an example of how to set up a simple supervisor:

```elixir
Copy code
defmodule MyApp.Supervisor do
  use Supervisor

  def start_link(_) do
```

```
  Supervisor.start_link(__MODULE__, [])
end

def init(_) do
  children = [
    {Task, fn -> IO.puts("Task running!") end}
  ]

  Supervisor.init(children, strategy: :one_for_one)
 end
end
```

In this example:

The start_link/1 function starts the supervisor process.
The init/1 function specifies the child processes and the restart strategy (:one_for_one in this case).

Fault Tolerance and Reliability

Supervisors are at the heart of Elixir's fault-tolerant design. By monitoring and restarting processes as necessary, they ensure that the application can recover from unexpected failures, without human intervention. This resilience is crucial for systems that must be highly available and responsive, even under heavy load or when encountering errors.

Isolation of Failures: When a child process fails, it is isolated from the rest of the system. Other processes can continue running without being affected.

Graceful Recovery: Supervisors allow for processes to recover without causing the entire system to fail, maintaining uptime.

Supervision Trees

In Elixir, supervisors are often organized into supervision trees—a hierarchical structure where supervisors can have their own child supervisors. This allows for modular error handling and recovery, where different parts of the system can have tailored supervision strategies.

For example:

A root supervisor might supervise a set of application components (e.g., database, web server, task manager).
Each component can have its own supervisor for managing its own processes.

This structure helps build applications that are resilient to failures and scale efficiently.

Best Practices for Using Supervisors

Keep Supervisors Small: Supervisors should have a small number of children to manage. Overloading a supervisor with too many processes can cause performance bottlenecks. Use Appropriate Restart Strategies: Choose the right restart strategy based on the relationship between child processes. For example, use one_for_one when child processes are independent and one_for_all when they are dependent on each other.

Monitor Long-Running Processes: Long-running or resource-intensive processes should be supervised carefully to ensure they are restarted promptly in case of failure. Hierarchical Supervision: Use a hierarchy of supervisors to create a fault-tolerant architecture where processes are grouped based on their purpose and dependencies.

Conclusion

Supervisors are essential in Elixir applications for building reliable, fault-tolerant systems. By leveraging supervisors and supervision strategies, developers can ensure that processes are continuously monitored and recovered in the event of failures. This helps to create resilient applications that can handle errors gracefully, ensuring minimal downtime and improved reliability in production environments.

## 7.2 Building Fault-Tolerant Systems

Elixir is designed with fault tolerance in mind, making it an ideal choice for building reliable, scalable, and resilient systems. Fault-tolerant systems are essential for applications that require high availability, minimal downtime, and the ability to recover from failures automatically. Elixir's concurrency model, based on the Actor Model, combined with its supervision system, allows developers to build applications that can withstand crashes and unexpected events without significant disruption.

### Core Principles of Fault-Tolerant Systems in Elixir

Isolation of Failures: In Elixir, each process is isolated from others. If one process crashes, it does not affect the rest of the system. This prevents cascading failures and allows the system to continue functioning even when individual components fail.

Process Monitoring and Restart: Processes in Elixir are lightweight and can be monitored by supervisors. If a process fails, the supervisor automatically restarts it according to predefined strategies. This ensures that the system can recover gracefully from crashes.

Supervision Trees: Supervisors in Elixir are structured in hierarchical trees, where a supervisor manages a set of child processes. If any child process fails, the supervisor can restart it, ensuring that the affected component is quickly restored without impacting the entire system. The ability to nest supervisors allows for scalable and modular fault tolerance.

Elixir's Fault-Tolerant Model

Elixir's fault tolerance model is centered around the concept of "Let it crash". This philosophy encourages designing processes to fail fast and cleanly, allowing supervisors to handle recovery. The idea is that instead of catching every possible error in the application, processes should be allowed to crash and then be restarted in a known, clean state by a supervisor.

This model is supported by:

Lightweight Processes: Each process in Elixir runs in its own isolated memory space, which means that errors in one process do not propagate to others.

Message Passing: Processes communicate via asynchronous message passing, which decouples them and prevents shared memory issues that could lead to complex bugs and failures.

Supervisor Trees: A hierarchical structure of supervisors and child processes that automatically recover from failures based on predefined strategies.

Key Components in Building Fault-Tolerant Systems

Supervisors: Supervisors monitor and manage child processes, ensuring that if a process crashes, it can be restarted automatically. There are different restart strategies to choose from, depending on how critical the failure is to the overall system.

One-for-One: Restarts only the crashed process.

One-for-All: Restarts all processes if one fails.

Rest-for-One: Restarts the crashed process and any processes started after it.

Error Handling: Rather than handling every error within a process, Elixir encourages the use of supervision to manage errors. This simplifies the code and promotes the "Let it crash" philosophy, where processes fail and recover without causing widespread disruptions.

Monitoring: Elixir processes can be monitored using Process.monitor/1, and supervisors can track the state of processes to detect failures. This monitoring helps in detecting errors early and triggering recovery strategies.

GenServer: GenServer is a key abstraction in Elixir that simplifies the creation of stateful processes. It is commonly used for building fault-tolerant systems because it provides built-in mechanisms for handling messages, errors, and crashes.

Designing for Fault Tolerance

When designing fault-tolerant systems in Elixir, consider the following principles:

Minimize Shared State: Avoid shared state between processes. Instead, use message passing to communicate between isolated processes. This ensures that one process's failure doesn't lead to inconsistent or corrupted shared state.

Identify Critical Components: Understand which parts of your system are most critical and need to be supervised with more robust fault-tolerance strategies. For example, a database connection pool should be supervised with a "One-for-All" strategy, while individual worker tasks might only need "One-for-One" supervision.

Graceful Degradation: In cases of failure, the system should degrade gracefully rather than crash completely. This can be achieved by using redundant processes, fallback mechanisms, and careful monitoring of critical services.

Use of Backoff and Retry Mechanisms: When building distributed systems, it's important to implement backoff and retry strategies when interacting with external services.

This helps prevent overwhelming resources and provides time for temporary issues to resolve.

Practical Techniques for Fault-Tolerant Systems

Monitoring and Alarming: Use Process.monitor/1 and GenServer to monitor processes and trigger alarms when they fail. This allows for proactive management and alerts when something goes wrong.

Self-Healing Systems: Design systems that automatically recover from failures. For example, if a process crashes, the supervisor restarts it, and if multiple processes fail in quick succession, the system should automatically pause or switch to a backup to prevent overload.

Dynamic Process Management: Use dynamic workers, such as task pools or worker pools, to distribute load efficiently across the system. The supervisor can scale the number of workers up or down depending on demand, ensuring that the system remains responsive under heavy load.

Load Balancing and Distribution: In distributed systems, load balancing is key to fault tolerance. Ensure that work is distributed evenly across nodes to prevent a single point of failure from impacting the entire system.

Real-World Applications of Fault-Tolerant Systems in Elixir

Web Servers: Elixir's Phoenix framework is widely used for building scalable and fault-tolerant web applications. The underlying process model allows Phoenix to handle large numbers of simultaneous connections efficiently while recovering gracefully from failures.

Telecommunications: Systems that need to handle high volumes of real-time data, such as telecommunications platforms, benefit from Elixir's lightweight processes and supervision trees, ensuring that failures in one part of the system don't bring down the entire service.

Distributed Systems: In microservices or distributed architectures, Elixir's ability to handle process failures and recovery ensures that communication between services can continue even when individual nodes or services experience issues.

Conclusion

Elixir's design principles and tools, including lightweight processes, supervisors, and message-passing concurrency, make it an excellent choice for building fault-tolerant systems. By leveraging these features, developers can create applications that automatically recover from failures, ensuring high availability and resilience. Fault-tolerant systems are essential for modern applications, and Elixir provides the tools to design them efficiently and effectively.

## 7.3 Designing Resilient Applications

Resilient applications are systems that can maintain continuous operation, even in the face of failures or unexpected events. These applications are designed to handle errors gracefully, recover from crashes automatically, and provide high availability without significant downtime. Elixir, with its robust concurrency model and fault-tolerant architecture, is an ideal language for building such resilient systems. By leveraging Elixir's strengths, developers can build applications that can handle high traffic, complex workflows, and unpredictable conditions without breaking down.

Core Principles of Resilience in Elixir

Fault Isolation: Elixir's processes are lightweight and isolated from each other. If one process crashes, it does not impact the others, preventing a single failure from taking down the entire system. This principle of isolation allows developers to build systems that can handle failures without significant disruption.

Self-Healing with Supervisors: Supervisors play a crucial role in making applications resilient. They monitor and restart processes that fail according to predefined strategies. This automatic recovery ensures that the system can return to normal operation quickly without manual intervention.

Concurrency and Scalability: Elixir's actor-based concurrency model enables the creation of numerous processes that operate independently and concurrently. This concurrency, combined with Elixir's ability to scale horizontally across multiple nodes, ensures that the application can handle increased load and recover from failures in specific parts of the system.

"Let it Crash" Philosophy: Elixir embraces the "Let it crash" philosophy, where processes are allowed to fail quickly and cleanly. Instead of trying to prevent errors within each process, Elixir encourages designers to let processes fail and rely on supervisors to manage recovery. This leads to simpler and more maintainable code.

Building Blocks of Resilient Applications

Supervision Trees: At the heart of resilience in Elixir is the supervision tree. A supervisor manages the lifecycle of its child processes, restarting them if they fail. The tree structure allows developers to build hierarchical systems where different parts of the application can be supervised with different strategies.

One-for-One: Only the crashed process is restarted.
One-for-All: If one process fails, all processes in the supervisor are restarted.
Rest-for-One: If a process fails, it and the subsequent processes are restarted.

This flexibility allows developers to apply the most appropriate restart strategy based on the application's architecture.

Lightweight Processes: Each process in Elixir is isolated and runs independently, making it easy to handle failures at a granular level. This isolation ensures that one process failure does not affect the rest of the system. For example, if a task worker crashes, other tasks can continue running without being affected.

Error Handling with try/catch and rescue: While Elixir encourages letting processes crash, it still provides error-handling mechanisms like try/catch and rescue for handling expected errors. These mechanisms can be used in specific cases where catching and recovering from an error is necessary. However, it is important to use these judiciously and not to rely on them for controlling normal program flow.

Designing for High Availability

To ensure that an Elixir application is highly available, there are several design patterns and strategies that can be implemented:

Replication and Clustering: Elixir's distributed nature allows applications to scale horizontally across multiple machines (or nodes). By clustering nodes together, Elixir applications can replicate their processes across multiple machines, ensuring that if one node goes down, the others can continue to serve requests.

Graceful Degradation: Instead of failing completely when an error occurs, resilient applications should degrade gracefully. This means the system may reduce functionality or provide fallback options but continues to operate. For instance, a web application might fall back to a cached version of a page if the database is temporarily unavailable.

Load Balancing: Load balancing across multiple processes and nodes helps to evenly distribute traffic and tasks. This prevents individual processes or machines from becoming overwhelmed and failing. In Elixir, load balancing can be achieved through distributed task workers or by using third-party tools for load distribution.

State Persistence and Recovery: In many systems, it is crucial to persist the state of the application in the event of a crash. Elixir provides several tools for persisting state, such as the

GenServer process, which can store data in memory and persist it to disk when necessary. This allows the system to recover its state upon restart.

Building Resilient Components

GenServer: The GenServer abstraction is commonly used to build stateful components in Elixir. It provides an easy way to manage state, handle synchronous and asynchronous messages, and ensure error handling is centralized. By combining GenServer with supervisors, we can build components that are both resilient and scalable.

Task and Worker Pools: For managing long-running or parallelizable tasks, you can use Elixir's Task module or worker pools. These allow for concurrent processing of tasks, ensuring that if one worker fails, others can continue processing. Worker pools can be dynamically adjusted based on load to maintain system performance.

Distributed Systems: When building large-scale applications, distributing processes across multiple nodes can improve both performance and fault tolerance. Elixir makes it easy to create distributed systems where processes can communicate across machines using message passing.

Rate Limiting and Backoff: Implementing rate-limiting mechanisms, such as exponential backoff, helps to prevent system overload in the event of failures or high traffic. By slowing down or temporarily halting operations, the system can recover without crashing or being overwhelmed.

Strategies for Resilient Elixir Applications

Monitor Critical Processes: Continuously monitor key components of the application. Elixir provides the Process.monitor/1 function, which allows processes to be monitored for failure. If a critical process fails, supervisors can take appropriate action, such as restarting the process or taking it offline for maintenance.

Avoid Blocking Operations: Blocking operations can cause bottlenecks, which may result in cascading failures across the system. By using non-blocking operations and asynchronous message passing, Elixir ensures that the system remains responsive and resilient under heavy load.

Self-Healing Systems with Circuit Breakers: You can implement circuit breakers in your application to detect when certain components are failing and temporarily isolate them from the rest of the system. This prevents overloaded or failing services from affecting other parts of the application.

Logging and Metrics: Implement robust logging and metrics collection to detect and diagnose issues early. Tools like Telemetry and Logger can help track performance, detect bottlenecks, and provide insights into system health.

Conclusion

Designing resilient applications with Elixir involves leveraging its powerful concurrency model, lightweight processes, and fault-tolerant features like supervisors and message passing. By adhering to principles such as fault isolation, graceful degradation, and high availability, developers can build systems that continue to function effectively under stress or after failures. Whether you're building distributed systems, web applications, or real-time services, Elixir provides the tools necessary to ensure your application remains robust, reliable, and highly available.

## Chapter 8
### Scalability and Distributed Systems

Scalability and the ability to handle large, distributed systems are core strengths of Elixir, making it an ideal choice for building high-performance applications that need to scale horizontally. Elixir's foundation on the Erlang virtual machine (BEAM) provides powerful features for building scalable and fault-tolerant systems, leveraging its lightweight process model and message-passing capabilities.

Scalability in Elixir

Elixir's lightweight processes allow for the efficient handling of a large number of concurrent tasks, which is crucial for building scalable systems. By distributing tasks across multiple processes, Elixir can handle increased load by adding more processes rather than relying on traditional threading or blocking mechanisms. This allows systems to scale vertically (on a single machine) and horizontally (across multiple machines or nodes) with minimal effort.

Key scalability features in Elixir include:

Lightweight Processes: Elixir processes are highly concurrent and isolated, with low memory overhead. This allows you to spawn millions of processes, which can efficiently handle tasks concurrently.

Fault Tolerance: Processes are isolated from one another, so failure in one process doesn't impact others. This ensures that the system remains resilient under high load, and individual process failures can be handled without downtime.

Load Balancing: Elixir enables load balancing by distributing tasks across processes or nodes, ensuring that no single process or machine is overwhelmed.

Distributed Systems in Elixir

Elixir's support for distributed systems is built into its core. Through the use of Erlang's distribution model, Elixir applications can run across multiple nodes, allowing processes to communicate seamlessly between machines. Elixir's ability to form clusters of nodes enables the development of applications that scale across different servers, handle more users, and process larger amounts of data.

Key aspects of distributed systems in Elixir include:

Node Clustering: Elixir nodes can be connected to form a cluster. Once connected, they can share and manage processes across multiple machines, facilitating the creation of distributed applications that are scalable and resilient.

Distributed Process Communication: Elixir uses message-passing to enable communication between processes, even when they reside on different nodes. This allows for easy scaling of applications without complex inter-thread communication mechanisms.

Hot Code Upgrades: Elixir inherits this feature from Erlang, enabling live system updates without downtime. This is especially valuable for distributed systems where uptime is critical.

Scalability Use Cases

Elixir is well-suited for a variety of use cases that require both scalability and distribution, including:

Real-time Applications: Applications like chat systems, notifications, and live data feeds, which need to handle many concurrent connections, benefit from Elixir's concurrency model.

Microservices: Elixir's distributed nature makes it easy to build microservices architectures, where each service can run on a separate node and communicate with others in a fault-tolerant manner.

Large-Scale Web Servers: With tools like Cowboy and Phoenix, Elixir can handle massive numbers of web requests concurrently, ensuring that web applications scale seamlessly with increasing demand.

In conclusion, Elixir's ability to scale horizontally and handle distributed workloads, combined with its fault-tolerant and concurrent design, makes it a powerful choice for building scalable, distributed systems that can meet the demands of modern applications.

8.1 Understanding Scalability in Elixir

Scalability refers to a system's ability to handle an increasing amount of work, or its potential to accommodate growth. In the context of Elixir, scalability is a key feature that makes it well-suited for building high-performance applications that need to handle large numbers of concurrent tasks or users. Elixir achieves scalability through its lightweight process model, its underlying Erlang VM (BEAM), and its support for both vertical and horizontal scaling.

Key Concepts of Scalability in Elixir

Lightweight Processes: Elixir uses the Erlang VM's lightweight process model, where each process is independent and isolated. These processes are much lighter than traditional threads, meaning that thousands or even millions of processes can be spawned without significant overhead. This enables Elixir applications to scale by creating a large number of concurrent processes to handle various tasks, such as user requests, background jobs, or real-time updates.

Concurrency Without Blocking: Elixir's concurrency model is based on message passing between processes, which do not block each other. This non-blocking architecture allows processes to run concurrently and independently, without waiting for each other. As a result, systems can handle a large volume of requests in parallel, enabling better resource utilization and performance under load.

Immutable Data: In Elixir, data is immutable, meaning once a piece of data is created, it cannot be changed. This immutability makes it easier to scale applications because processes can safely share and communicate data without the risk of race conditions or data corruption. When a process needs to update its state, it creates a new version of the data, ensuring that previous versions remain intact and accessible to other processes.

Fault Isolation: Elixir's approach to scalability is built on the concept of fault isolation. If one process fails, it does not affect others. This allows individual processes to be restarted without bringing down the entire system. With tools like supervisors, Elixir ensures that processes that crash are automatically restarted, allowing the system to recover and continue handling tasks without interruption. This isolation makes scaling easier and more reliable because failure in one part of the system doesn't ripple through the entire application.

Message-Passing Concurrency: Elixir's processes communicate via message passing, which means that each process has its own mailbox to receive messages and send responses. This approach allows Elixir applications to scale naturally, as processes can run independently on different CPUs or even different machines without needing to share memory or manage complex locking mechanisms.

Types of Scalability in Elixir

Vertical Scaling: Vertical scaling refers to increasing the resources of a single machine, such as adding more CPU cores or memory. Elixir can take full advantage of multi-core processors by distributing processes across different cores. The BEAM automatically manages this distribution, ensuring that each process runs on the most available core, improving performance without any special configuration. However, while Elixir can take advantage of vertical scaling, it is often more efficient to scale horizontally.

Horizontal Scaling: Horizontal scaling involves adding more machines (nodes) to a system to distribute the load. Elixir makes horizontal scaling easy by allowing multiple nodes (computers) to form a cluster, where processes can run on different machines while still communicating seamlessly.

This clustering allows Elixir applications to scale across many nodes, increasing both computational power and fault tolerance. The ability to distribute processes across machines without complex setup is one of Elixir's biggest strengths in building highly scalable systems.

Scalability Features in Elixir

Node Clustering: Elixir supports distributed systems through its node clustering feature. By connecting multiple nodes (machines) together, Elixir processes can communicate across nodes as if they were on the same machine. This makes it possible to scale applications beyond a single server, distributing workloads and balancing resources across multiple machines to handle increased traffic or data.

Task and Process Distribution: Tasks and processes in Elixir can be distributed dynamically across multiple nodes. By using the Task module, Elixir allows you to easily spawn concurrent tasks that can run on different machines, making it simple to parallelize operations and improve throughput.

Load Balancing: As the number of processes grows, Elixir applications can implement load balancing to distribute workloads evenly across available resources. This is often done by clustering nodes and allowing them to share tasks efficiently, ensuring no single node is overwhelmed with work.

Distributed State Management: Elixir can manage state across distributed processes by using techniques like GenServer or external tools such as distributed databases or key-value stores. This allows Elixir to maintain consistency and high availability across nodes while handling increased traffic or load.

Challenges and Best Practices for Scalability

Network Latency: While horizontal scaling can distribute the workload, it introduces the challenge of network latency between nodes. Elixir handles this by using lightweight messaging and optimizing communication between distributed processes. However, developers must be mindful of the overhead involved in communication between distant nodes, especially as systems grow larger.

State Management: In distributed systems, managing the state consistently across nodes can become challenging. Elixir offers tools like GenServer for maintaining local state, but for large-scale systems, external solutions like distributed databases or caching systems might be necessary to ensure consistency.

Monitoring and Performance Tuning: As systems scale, monitoring performance and ensuring that resources are being utilized efficiently becomes essential. Elixir provides excellent tools for tracking processes and monitoring system performance, such as Telemetry and Logger. These tools help developers identify bottlenecks, diagnose issues, and fine-tune the application for better scalability.

Conclusion

Scalability is one of the most important features of Elixir, allowing developers to build applications that can handle a massive number of concurrent processes, scale across multiple machines, and recover gracefully from failures. By leveraging Elixir's lightweight processes, message-passing concurrency, fault isolation, and distributed system capabilities, developers can create highly scalable, reliable systems that grow as needed. Whether scaling vertically on a single machine or horizontally across many nodes, Elixir provides the tools and architecture to build systems capable of handling even the most demanding workloads.

## 8.2 Building Distributed Applications with Elixir

Building distributed applications with Elixir is a powerful approach to developing systems that can scale seamlessly, handle large numbers of concurrent tasks, and remain resilient in the face of failures. Elixir's architecture, built on the Erlang Virtual Machine (BEAM), provides built-in support for distributed computing, making it a natural choice for systems that need to operate across multiple nodes (machines) and maintain high availability.

Key Concepts in Building Distributed Applications with Elixir

Nodes and Clusters: Elixir applications can run on multiple nodes, where each node is essentially an instance of the Elixir runtime (a machine or process running the Elixir language). Nodes are connected to form a cluster, allowing distributed processes to communicate seamlessly as if they were on the same machine. Nodes in a cluster can share workloads, monitor each other, and handle failure recovery.

Creating Nodes: Each Elixir node is identified by a unique name, which is typically specified when the application starts. Nodes can be connected to form a cluster by specifying a list of nodes to connect to.

Node Communication: Once connected, nodes can communicate directly by sending messages to processes on other nodes, without the need for complex setup. Elixir abstracts away much of the complexity of distributed computing, allowing for easier communication between processes running on different machines.

Distributed Process Communication: In a distributed Elixir application, processes communicate with each other using message passing. The BEAM virtual machine automatically handles the communication between processes running on different nodes in the cluster. This allows for seamless interaction across the network with minimal latency.

Message Passing: Processes on different nodes can send and receive messages through the same mechanism used for local communication. Elixir's message-passing model abstracts the underlying network details, making distributed communication appear as simple as sending a message between local processes.

Process Migration: Elixir also allows processes to migrate from one node to another. This can be useful when distributing tasks or balancing workloads across different machines.

Fault Tolerance in Distributed Systems: Fault tolerance is a crucial feature of Elixir's distributed system model. Elixir is designed to handle failures gracefully, ensuring that an application can continue functioning even if individual components fail. This is achieved through process isolation, supervision trees, and automatic recovery mechanisms.

Process Isolation: Each process in Elixir is isolated from others, which means that a failure in one process doesn't affect the others. This isolation makes it easier to detect and recover from failures without interrupting the entire application.

Supervision Trees: Supervisors are special processes that monitor other processes and restart them if they fail. In a distributed system, supervisors can monitor processes on remote nodes and restart them as needed, ensuring system resilience.

Self-Healing: When a process fails, supervisors can automatically restart it, which allows the system to "heal" itself without human intervention. This approach is vital in distributed systems, where network issues or node failures are inevitable.

Consistency and Distributed State: Managing state across distributed nodes can be challenging, especially when the system needs to remain consistent and available across machines. Elixir offers several strategies to manage state in a distributed environment.

GenServer: The GenServer behavior is commonly used to manage state in Elixir applications. In a distributed system, you can have GenServer processes running on different nodes to handle different parts of the state. These processes can interact and coordinate to ensure consistency across the system.

Distributed Databases: For large-scale applications, distributed databases (such as Riak, Cassandra, or even Elixir's own ETS) can be used to store state across multiple nodes. These databases ensure that data is replicated and available across the cluster.

Eventual Consistency: In many distributed systems, achieving immediate consistency can be difficult due to network latency or partitioning. Elixir's distributed systems often rely on eventual consistency, where updates to state are propagated across nodes over time, ensuring that all nodes eventually reach the same state.

Building a Simple Distributed Elixir Application

Setting Up Nodes: To begin building a distributed application in Elixir, you first need to create multiple nodes. This can be done by specifying a name for each node when starting the Elixir shell (iex).

bash
Copy code
```
# Start the first node
$ iex --sname node1@localhost

# Start the second node
$ iex --sname node2@localhost
```

Once the nodes are started, you can connect them to form a cluster.

elixir
Copy code
# On node1
Node.connect(:node2@localhost)

Now, both nodes are part of the same cluster and can communicate with each other.

Spawning Processes Across Nodes: You can spawn processes on different nodes in the cluster and have them communicate with each other.

elixir
Copy code
# On node1
pid = spawn(:node2@localhost, fn -> IO.puts "Hello from node2" end)

This example spawns a process on node2, which prints a message to the console.

Handling Distributed State: Let's say you want to store and share state across nodes. You can use GenServer processes to manage distributed state.

```elixir
Copy code
# On node1
defmodule Counter do
  use GenServer

  def start_link(initial_value) do
      GenServer.start_link(__MODULE__, initial_value,
  name: :counter)
  end

  def init(initial_value) do
   {:ok, initial_value}
  end

  def increment do
   GenServer.cast(:counter, :increment)
  end

  def handle_cast(:increment, state) do
   {:noreply, state + 1}
  end
end
```

You can spawn the Counter process on one node and interact with it from other nodes in the cluster.

Supervisors in Distributed Systems:

Supervisors can be used to monitor processes running on different nodes and ensure that they are restarted if they fail. This can be done by defining a supervisor tree in Elixir and assigning the processes to be supervised.

Challenges in Distributed Elixir Systems

Network Latency: Communication between nodes over a network can introduce latency. Elixir handles this by using lightweight message-passing and efficient network protocols, but it's important to design applications with the assumption that network delays can occur.

Partitioning and Availability: In a distributed system, network partitions may occur, causing some nodes to become unreachable. Elixir's "let it crash" philosophy and automatic recovery mechanisms help the system remain available even when nodes temporarily fail or are partitioned.

Consistency: Maintaining consistency across distributed nodes can be challenging, especially in systems where data is replicated across multiple locations. Elixir developers typically adopt eventual consistency models or use distributed databases designed for high availability.

Conclusion

Building distributed applications with Elixir leverages its strengths in concurrency, fault tolerance, and scalability. With Elixir's native support for nodes, clustering, message-passing, and process isolation, developers can easily design applications that span multiple machines, handle large volumes of traffic, and recover from failures without manual intervention. Whether you're building a real-time chat system, a microservices architecture, or a highly available web application, Elixir's robust distributed computing capabilities make it an ideal choice for modern distributed systems.

8.3 Leveraging BEAM for Concurrent Systems

The BEAM (Bogdan/Björn's Erlang Abstract Machine) is the runtime system that powers Elixir and Erlang. It is specifically designed to handle massive concurrency, fault tolerance, and distributed systems. BEAM provides an efficient, highly concurrent, and fault-tolerant environment for building scalable applications. In this section, we'll explore how BEAM enables developers to build concurrent systems and how Elixir leverages BEAM to manage concurrency in a more effective and efficient way.

Understanding BEAM's Concurrency Model

The BEAM virtual machine's concurrency model is based on lightweight processes that run concurrently but independently of each other. These processes are not tied to operating system threads and are extremely lightweight compared to traditional threads. This allows Elixir to handle millions of concurrent processes efficiently, which is crucial for building highly concurrent systems.

Lightweight Processes:

Each BEAM process is a tiny unit of execution with its own state, mailbox, and message-passing system. BEAM processes are managed by the BEAM scheduler, which distributes the execution of processes across available CPU cores.

Since these processes are isolated and don't share memory, there is no need for locks or mutexes to synchronize access to shared data. This isolation eliminates many of the common problems associated with multithreading, such as race conditions and deadlocks.

Message Passing:

Communication between processes in BEAM is done through message passing, where one process sends a message to another. This design is fundamental to the actor model of computation, which underpins Elixir's concurrency model.

Message passing in BEAM is asynchronous, meaning the sender doesn't block while waiting for a response. Instead, the recipient process handles the message in its own time, making BEAM highly efficient in handling concurrent tasks.

No Shared State:

BEAM processes do not share memory or state. This ensures that each process is independent, avoiding the complexities of shared-memory concurrency.

If a process needs to communicate its state to another process, it sends a message with the relevant data. This promotes immutability and makes the system easier to reason about.

Concurrency in Elixir: Built on BEAM

Elixir builds on BEAM's powerful concurrency model to provide developers with a rich set of tools to create concurrent applications. Let's dive into how Elixir takes full advantage of BEAM for managing concurrency.

Elixir's Processes:

In Elixir, a "process" is a lightweight thread of execution managed by BEAM. These processes can be created, monitored, and interacted with using built-in Elixir functions.

You can spawn a process using the spawn function, which creates a new process and executes the given function within that process.

elixir

Copy code

```
# Creating a process in Elixir
spawn(fn -> IO.puts("Hello from a process!") end)
```

Concurrency with Task:

Elixir simplifies concurrency management with the Task module. Tasks are a higher-level abstraction over BEAM processes, designed for concurrent execution of functions.

Tasks can be asynchronous or synchronous, making them a flexible tool for building concurrent applications.

elixir

Copy code

```
# Asynchronous task
Task.async(fn -> IO.puts("Running in a separate process!") end)

# Synchronous task (waits for completion)
Task.await(Task.async(fn -> 42 end))
```

Managing Concurrency with GenServer:

One of the most powerful concurrency abstractions in Elixir is the GenServer (generic server). A GenServer is a process that manages its internal state and provides a set of functions for interacting with other processes.

The GenServer module makes it easy to spawn processes that can handle requests and manage state concurrently. This is ideal for building services such as databases, stateful services, and other long-running processes.

```elixir
Copy code
defmodule Counter do
  use GenServer

  # Client API
  def increment(pid) do
    GenServer.cast(pid, :increment)
  end

  def get(pid) do
    GenServer.call(pid, :get)
  end
```

```elixir
# Server API
def init(initial_value) do
  {:ok, initial_value}
end

def handle_cast(:increment, state) do
  {:noreply, state + 1}
end

def handle_call(:get, _from, state) do
  {:reply, state, state}
  end
end

# Start the GenServer
{:ok, pid} = GenServer.start_link(Counter, 0)

# Interact with the GenServer
Counter.increment(pid)
Counter.get(pid)
G
```

enServer processes are highly efficient for handling concurrent state management and making asynchronous requests to and from other processes.

Handling Large Numbers of Concurrent Processes

BEAM's lightweight process model allows Elixir to handle millions of processes concurrently. This is a key advantage when designing systems that need to scale efficiently, such as real-time applications, web servers, and messaging systems.

Scalability:

BEAM can run millions of lightweight processes across multiple CPU cores. These processes are managed by the BEAM scheduler, which is responsible for efficiently distributing work across available resources.
Elixir developers can build highly scalable systems without worrying about the overhead of traditional thread management or complex locking mechanisms.

Cooperative Scheduling:

BEAM uses a cooperative scheduling model where processes yield control to the scheduler voluntarily. This ensures that all processes get a fair share of the CPU time and avoids issues like thread starvation.

Since the scheduler is highly optimized, Elixir applications can handle large numbers of concurrent processes without significant performance degradation.

Fault Tolerance in Concurrent Systems

Elixir's concurrency model, built on BEAM, also provides excellent fault tolerance capabilities. The "let it crash" philosophy and process isolation ensure that failures in one process do not affect the entire system.

Process Isolation:

Each process in Elixir is isolated from others, meaning that a failure in one process (such as a crash) does not bring down the entire system. This is fundamental for building resilient, fault-tolerant systems.

Supervision Trees:

Supervisors are processes that monitor other processes. If a process crashes, the supervisor can restart it, ensuring the system remains functional.

Supervisors can be organized into supervision trees, where higher-level supervisors manage lower-level supervisors, creating a hierarchical fault-tolerance structure.

Conclusion

BEAM's concurrency model is one of the core strengths of Elixir, enabling the creation of highly concurrent, scalable, and fault-tolerant systems. By leveraging lightweight processes, message passing, and process isolation, Elixir builds on BEAM's robust foundation to offer developers a simple yet powerful way to handle concurrency. Whether you're building a real-time messaging app, a distributed service, or a fault-tolerant web application, BEAM's concurrency capabilities make Elixir an excellent choice for concurrent systems.

# PART IV: ADVANCED FUNCTIONAL PROGRAMMING TECHNIQUES

## Chapter 9
### Metaprogramming with Macros

Metaprogramming refers to the ability of a program to manipulate, modify, or generate code during compilation or runtime. In Elixir, macros are the primary tool for metaprogramming, enabling developers to extend the language's syntax and behavior in powerful ways.

What Are Macros?

A macro is a function that operates on the abstract syntax tree (AST) of the code before it is compiled. Unlike regular functions, which work on values at runtime, macros work at compile-time and can generate or modify code.

Macros allow Elixir developers to:

Define new control structures or domain-specific languages (DSLs).

Optimize code by removing repetitive patterns.

Abstract complex logic to make code more readable and maintainable.

How Macros Work in Elixir

When a macro is called, it receives code as input, manipulates the code in the form of the AST, and returns new code. This new code is then injected into the program before compilation.

Example of a simple macro:

```elixir
Copy code
defmodule MyMacros do
  defmacro say_hello do
    IO.puts "Hello from macro!"
  end
end

# Usage
defmodule MyApp do
```

```
  require MyMacros
  MyMacros.say_hello()
end
```

In this example, the macro say_hello generates an IO.puts statement at compile-time.

Use Cases for Macros

Code generation: Macros can be used to generate repetitive code, such as defining getter and setter functions for struct fields.

Domain-Specific Languages (DSLs): By creating custom macros, developers can create new DSLs tailored to specific use cases, improving readability and expressiveness.

Optimizing performance: Macros allow you to optimize parts of the code by unrolling loops or pre-calculating values at compile-time.

Conclusion

Macros are a powerful tool in Elixir, enabling developers to enhance their applications with custom language extensions and code generation. By manipulating code at compile-time, macros offer a flexible way to reduce boilerplate, improve performance, and create more expressive DSLs. However, they should be used carefully, as they can make code more complex and harder to debug.

## 9.1 Introduction to Metaprogramming

Metaprogramming is the art of writing programs that can manipulate, generate, or transform code during compilation or runtime. It allows developers to extend the capabilities of a programming language, automate repetitive tasks, and create more expressive and concise code. In Elixir, metaprogramming is a fundamental feature, made possible by the language's powerful macro system.

What Is Metaprogramming?

At its core, metaprogramming involves working with the abstract syntax tree (AST) of a program. The AST is a representation of code in a structured format that the compiler can understand. By accessing and manipulating this representation, developers can create new behaviors, optimize existing ones, or generate dynamic code.

Metaprogramming is often used for:

Language Extensions: Adding custom syntax or features to a language.
Code Abstraction: Reducing redundancy and boilerplate in codebases.
Domain-Specific Languages (DSLs): Designing specialized syntaxes for specific tasks or industries.
Compile-Time Optimization: Transforming code during compilation to improve performance.

Metaprogramming in Elixir

Elixir's metaprogramming capabilities revolve around macros. Unlike functions, which operate on values at runtime, macros operate on the AST at compile-time. This means macros can inject, modify, or transform code before the program is executed.

For example, consider a simple Elixir function versus a macro:

```elixir
Copy code
# Function example
def greet(name), do: "Hello, #{name}!"

# Macro example
defmacro greet_macro(name) do
  quote do
    "Hello, #{unquote(name)}!"
  end
end
```

The macro greet_macro generates code dynamically, which is injected into the program during compilation. This flexibility makes macros a powerful tool for metaprogramming.

Advantages of Metaprogramming

Code Reduction: Metaprogramming eliminates repetitive code by dynamically generating it.

Custom Extensions: Developers can introduce new language constructs tailored to their specific needs.

Enhanced Readability: By encapsulating complex logic within macros, code becomes more concise and easier to understand.

Improved Productivity: Automation of repetitive tasks allows developers to focus on solving higher-level problems.

Challenges of Metaprogramming

While metaprogramming offers significant benefits, it also comes with potential pitfalls:

Complexity: Generated code can be harder to understand and debug compared to manually written code.

Performance Overhead: Poorly designed macros can increase compilation time or generate inefficient code.

Maintainability: Excessive use of metaprogramming can make codebases harder to maintain, especially for teams unfamiliar with its constructs.

Conclusion

Metaprogramming is a powerful feature in Elixir that enables developers to go beyond the standard capabilities of the language. By manipulating code at the AST level, developers can create custom extensions, reduce boilerplate, and optimize performance. However, it's essential to use metaprogramming judiciously to balance its benefits with the potential complexity it introduces.

## 9.2 Writing Macros in Elixir

Macros in Elixir are powerful tools that allow developers to generate and manipulate code at compile-time. They operate on the abstract syntax tree (AST) of the code, enabling the creation of custom language constructs, optimizations, and dynamic code generation. Writing macros effectively requires a clear understanding of their syntax, purpose, and behavior.

What Are Macros in Elixir?

A macro is a special type of function that takes code as input, transforms it, and returns new code to be compiled. Unlike regular functions, which work with values at runtime, macros operate on code structures during the compilation phase.

Macros are defined using the defmacro keyword and typically use the quote and unquote mechanisms to handle code fragments.

Syntax for Defining Macros

Here is a basic example of a macro:

```elixir
Copy code
defmodule MyMacros do
  defmacro greet(name) do
    quote do
      "Hello, #{unquote(name)}!"
    end
  end
end
```

In this example:

defmacro: Defines the macro.

quote: Returns the AST of the code within it.

unquote: Injects the evaluated value of a variable or expression into the quoted code.

Using Macros

Macros must be explicitly required before use. Here's how the above macro can be used:

```elixir
Copy code
defmodule MyApp do
  require MyMacros

  def example do
    IO.puts MyMacros.greet("Alice")
  end
end
```

When MyMacros.greet("Alice") is invoked, the macro generates the code "Hello, Alice!" during compilation.

Key Concepts in Writing Macros

Quoting and Unquoting:

quote captures code as a data structure (AST).

unquote injects evaluated expressions into the quoted code.

Example:

```elixir
Copy code
quote do
  IO.puts "Hello"
end
```

Hygiene: Macros in Elixir are hygienic, meaning variables introduced in macros do not clash with those in the caller's context. If necessary, developers can use Macro.var/2 to bypass this.

Pattern Matching: Macros often use pattern matching to process and transform code.

Best Practices for Writing Macros

Keep Macros Simple: Avoid complex logic in macros to maintain readability and debugging ease.

Use Functions When Possible: Only use macros for tasks that cannot be achieved with functions, such as code generation or adding syntax.

Comment and Document: Clearly explain what a macro does, as its behavior may not be immediately obvious.

Test Extensively: Ensure macros produce the expected output in all scenarios to avoid introducing bugs.

Example: Defining a Custom Control Structure

Here's an example of a macro that implements a simple unless construct:

```elixir
Copy code
defmodule MyMacros do
  defmacro my_unless(condition, do: block) do
    quote do
      if !unquote(condition) do
        unquote(block)
      end
    end
  end
end
```

```
end

# Usage
defmodule MyApp do
  require MyMacros

  def test do
    MyMacros.my_unless true do
      IO.puts "This won't print."
    end
  end
end
```

This macro rewrites the code into an if statement, demonstrating how macros can create custom control structures.

Conclusion

Macros in Elixir are a cornerstone of its metaprogramming capabilities, providing developers with a way to extend the language and simplify complex code patterns. While macros are powerful, they should be used judiciously to avoid introducing unnecessary complexity or performance issues. By following best practices and leveraging Elixir's macro system effectively, developers can create expressive and efficient code.

## 9.3 Practical Applications of Metaprogramming

Metaprogramming in Elixir enables developers to extend the language, automate repetitive tasks, and create more expressive, efficient, and maintainable code. By leveraging macros and manipulating the abstract syntax tree (AST), developers can address complex programming challenges with elegant solutions. Below are some practical applications of metaprogramming in Elixir.

### 1. Creating Domain-Specific Languages (DSLs)

Elixir's metaprogramming capabilities make it ideal for building DSLs, which are specialized syntaxes tailored for specific tasks. For example:

Phoenix Framework uses DSLs to define routes (get "/page", PageController).

Ecto employs DSLs for query building and schema definitions.

With macros, developers can design intuitive and readable DSLs to simplify interactions within their applications.

Example:

```elixir
Copy code
defmodule HTMLBuilder do
  defmacro tag(name, do: content) do
    quote do

"<#{unquote(name)}>#{unquote(content)}</#{unquote(name)}>"
    end
  end
end


# Usage
require HTMLBuilder

HTMLBuilder.tag(:div, do: "Hello, World!")
# Outputs: "<div>Hello, World!</div>"
```

## 2. Eliminating Boilerplate Code

Macros can generate repetitive code automatically, reducing redundancy and improving maintainability.

Example: Generating CRUD functions:

elixir
Copy code
```elixir
defmodule MyCRUD do
  defmacro create_crud(module_name) do
    quote do
            def create(data), do: IO.puts("Creating #{unquote(module_name)}: #{inspect(data)}")
            def read(id), do: IO.puts("Reading #{unquote(module_name)} with ID: #{id}")
          def update(id, data), do: IO.puts("Updating #{unquote(module_name)}: #{id} -> #{inspect(data)}")
            def delete(id), do: IO.puts("Deleting #{unquote(module_name)} with ID: #{id}")
    end
  end
end
```

# Usage

```elixir
defmodule UserModule do
  require MyCRUD
  MyCRUD.create_crud(:user)
end
```

3. Enhancing Testing

Metaprogramming simplifies testing by generating test cases dynamically. For example, creating parameterized tests or repetitive assertions can be streamlined with macros.

Example:

```elixir
elixir
Copy code
defmodule TestHelper do
  defmacro generate_tests(test_cases) do
    for {name, result} <- test_cases do
      quote do
        test "#{unquote(name)}" do
          assert unquote(result)
        end
      end
    end
  end
end
```

```
end

# Usage
defmodule ExampleTest do
  use ExUnit.Case
  require TestHelper

  TestHelper.generate_tests([
    {"test one", 1 + 1 == 2},
    {"test two", String.length("hello") == 5}
  ])
end
```

4. Dynamic Code Generation

Macros allow the generation of code based on compile-time inputs, enabling highly customizable behavior without runtime overhead.

Example: Defining struct fields dynamically:

```
elixir
Copy code
defmodule StructGenerator do
  defmacro generate_struct(fields) do
```

```
  quote do
    defstruct unquote(fields)
  end
 end
end

# Usage
defmodule MyStruct do
 require StructGenerator
 StructGenerator.generate_struct([:name, :age, :email])
end
```

5. Compile-Time Validations

Macros can enforce validations during compilation, catching errors early. For instance, a macro can validate function arguments or configuration values at compile-time to prevent runtime issues.

Example: Validating environment variables:

```
elixir
Copy code
defmodule EnvValidator do
 defmacro validate_env(var) do
```

```
  if System.get_env(var) do
    :ok
  else
    raise "#{var} is not set in the environment."
  end
 end
end
```

```
# Usage
require EnvValidator
EnvValidator.validate_env("DATABASE_URL")
```

6. Optimizing Performance

Metaprogramming can optimize performance by unrolling loops or generating specialized code paths. This reduces runtime overhead by handling computations during compilation.

Example: Generating mathematical functions:

```elixir
Copy code
defmodule MathMacros do
  defmacro generate_power_functions(max) do
```

```elixir
    for i <- 1..max do
      quote do
          def unquote(:"power_#{i}")(x), do: :math.pow(x,
unquote(i))
      end
     end
   end
end

# Usage
defmodule MyMath do
  require MathMacros
  MathMacros.generate_power_functions(3)
end
```

Conclusion

Metaprogramming in Elixir is a transformative tool that empowers developers to simplify codebases, create expressive DSLs, optimize performance, and catch errors early. While it introduces powerful capabilities, it should be used judiciously to maintain code clarity and ensure long-term maintainability. With proper planning and thoughtful design, metaprogramming can elevate Elixir applications to new levels of flexibility and efficiency.

## Chapter 10
## Working with Streams and Lazy Evaluation

Elixir's support for streams and lazy evaluation allows developers to work efficiently with large or potentially infinite data collections by processing elements only as needed. This approach is memory-efficient and avoids unnecessary computations, making it ideal for scenarios like file processing, API data streams, or long-running computations.

Streams in Elixir

A stream in Elixir represents a composable, lazy sequence of elements. Instead of generating all elements upfront, a stream produces them on demand. The Stream module provides functions for creating and manipulating streams.

Example of creating a stream:

elixir

Copy code

```
stream = Stream.map(1..10, fn x -> x * 2 end)
```

Here, no computation occurs until the stream is consumed.

Lazy Evaluation

Lazy evaluation ensures that operations on a stream are deferred until the data is explicitly needed. This allows chaining multiple transformations without generating intermediate collections, conserving memory.

Example of consuming a stream:

elixir
Copy code

```
stream = Stream.map(1..10, &(&1 * 2))
Enum.to_list(stream) # Triggers evaluation and returns [2, 4, 6, 8, 10, 12, 14, 16, 18, 20]
```

Common Stream Operations

Transformations:

Use functions like Stream.map/2 or Stream.filter/2 for lazy transformations.

Example:

elixir

Copy code

```
Stream.filter(1..10, fn x -> rem(x, 2) == 0 end)
```

Infinite Streams:

Generate infinite sequences with Stream.iterate/2 or Stream.cycle/1.

Example:

elixir

Copy code

```
Stream.iterate(0, &(&1 + 1)) |> Enum.take(5)
```

File and I/O Streaming:

Process large files line by line using File.stream!/1.

Example:

elixir

Copy code

```
File.stream!("large_file.txt")
|> Stream.map(&String.trim/1)
|> Enum.take(10)
```

Advantages of Using Streams

Memory Efficiency: Handles large datasets without loading everything into memory.

Performance: Processes data incrementally, avoiding the overhead of intermediate collections.

Composability: Simplifies complex pipelines by chaining transformations.

Conclusion

Working with streams and lazy evaluation in Elixir enhances both performance and resource utilization. By leveraging streams, developers can build scalable applications that handle vast amounts of data efficiently while maintaining a clean and composable code structure.

10.1 What Are Streams?

Streams in Elixir represent lazy, composable enumerables that allow for processing data incrementally and on-demand. Unlike lists, which are eagerly evaluated and require all elements to be computed and stored in memory upfront, streams delay computation until their elements are explicitly accessed or consumed.

Key Characteristics of Streams
Laziness:

Streams do not evaluate or generate elements until required. This makes them memory-efficient, especially when working with large datasets or infinite sequences.

Composability:

Streams can be easily transformed and combined using functions from the Stream module, enabling the creation of powerful data pipelines.

Efficiency:

By deferring computations and processing elements as needed, streams minimize memory usage and avoid unnecessary work.

How Streams Work

Streams use enumerable protocols, just like lists, maps, and other collections in Elixir. However, they differ in that they do not store data but instead define a sequence of operations to apply when the stream is eventually consumed.

Example:

elixir
Copy code
```
stream = Stream.map(1..10, fn x -> x * 2 end)
# At this point, no computation has occurred.
Enum.to_list(stream)  # Triggers evaluation and produces
[2, 4, 6, 8, 10, 12, 14, 16, 18, 20]
```

Creating Streams

From Existing Enumerables:

Transform an enumerable into a stream using Stream.map/2, Stream.filter/2, and similar functions.

elixir
Copy code
```
Stream.map(1..5, &(&1 * 2))
```

Infinite Streams:

Use Stream.cycle/1, Stream.iterate/2, or Stream.repeatedly/1 to create streams with an infinite number of elements.

elixir
Copy code
```
Stream.iterate(1, &(&1 + 1))
|> Enum.take(5) # [1, 2, 3, 4, 5]
```

From File or I/O:

Stream data from files or other I/O sources using File.stream!/1.

elixir
Copy code
```
File.stream!("example.txt")
|> Stream.map(&String.trim/1)
|> Enum.to_list()
```

Benefits of Streams

Memory Conservation: Suitable for processing large datasets without loading everything into memory.

Improved Performance: Avoids unnecessary computations by evaluating only when needed.

Simplified Pipelines: Stream functions are composable, making it easy to build readable and modular code.

Conclusion

Streams are a powerful tool in Elixir for handling data efficiently. By enabling lazy evaluation and incremental processing, they provide developers with a way to build scalable, high-performance applications while conserving resources.

10.2 Implementing Lazy Evaluation

Lazy evaluation in Elixir refers to deferring the computation of values until they are explicitly needed. This approach optimizes resource usage by processing data incrementally and avoiding unnecessary calculations. Streams are Elixir's primary mechanism for implementing lazy evaluation, allowing developers to handle large datasets or infinite sequences efficiently.

How Lazy Evaluation Works

Lazy evaluation operates by defining a sequence of computations but not executing them immediately. Instead, the computations are stored as a pipeline of operations, which are only executed when the result is required.

Example:

elixir
Copy code
```
stream = Stream.map(1..10, fn x -> x * 2 end)
# At this stage, no values are calculated.
Enum.to_list(stream)  # Triggers computation and produces
[2, 4, 6, 8, 10, 12, 14, 16, 18, 20]
```

Key Steps to Implement Lazy Evaluation

Create Streams:
Use the Stream module to define a lazy enumerable.

elixir

Copy code
```
stream = Stream.filter(1..10, fn x -> rem(x, 2) == 0 end)
```

Compose Operations:

Chain multiple transformations without computing intermediate results.

elixir
Copy code
```
stream = Stream.map(1..10, &(&1 * 2)) |> Stream.filter(&(&1 > 10))
```

Consume the Stream:

Evaluate the lazy computations using Enum functions like Enum.to_list/1, Enum.take/2, or other terminal operations.

elixir
Copy code
```
Enum.to_list(stream)  # Triggers all computations in the pipeline.
```

Common Scenarios for Lazy Evaluation

Processing Large Data:

Handle datasets too large to fit into memory by processing them in chunks.

elixir
Copy code
```
File.stream!("large_file.txt")
|> Stream.map(&String.trim/1)
|> Enum.take(10)
```

Infinite Data Generation:

Generate infinite sequences, such as Fibonacci numbers or number iterations, using functions like Stream.iterate/2.

elixir
Copy code
```
Stream.iterate(1, &(&1 + 1))
|> Enum.take(5) # [1, 2, 3, 4, 5]
```
Efficient Data Pipelines:
Build complex pipelines where only the necessary elements are computed.

elixir

```
Copy code
1..10
|> Stream.map(&(&1 * 2))
|> Stream.filter(&(&1 > 10))
|> Enum.to_list()
```

Benefits of Lazy Evaluation

Memory Efficiency:
Processes data incrementally without loading the entire dataset into memory.

Performance Optimization:

Avoids unnecessary computations, focusing only on required elements.

Improved Code Clarity:

Enables the creation of modular and composable pipelines for complex data transformations.

Best Practices

Use lazy evaluation for large or infinite datasets.

Ensure streams are consumed eventually to trigger computations.
Be mindful of chaining too many operations, as excessive lazy evaluations can become difficult to debug.

Conclusion

Lazy evaluation is a powerful paradigm in Elixir that allows for efficient and scalable data processing. By using streams, developers can handle large datasets, generate infinite sequences, and build robust data pipelines while conserving resources and improving performance.

10.3 Optimizing Performance with Streams

Streams in Elixir are a powerful tool for optimizing performance, especially when working with large datasets or computationally expensive operations. By leveraging lazy evaluation, streams allow developers to process data incrementally and reduce memory usage, resulting in faster and more efficient applications.

Key Benefits of Streams for Performance

Lazy Evaluation:

Operations are deferred until the data is explicitly needed, avoiding unnecessary calculations and improving runtime efficiency.

Memory Efficiency:

Streams process data element by element rather than loading entire collections into memory, which is ideal for large or infinite datasets.

Composable Pipelines:

Streams enable the creation of modular and efficient data processing pipelines, minimizing intermediate data structures.

Optimizing with Streams: Best Practices

Use Streams for Large Datasets:

For collections like large ranges or files, streams reduce memory overhead.

Example:

```elixir
Copy code
File.stream!("large_file.txt")
|> Stream.map(&String.trim/1)
|> Stream.filter(&String.starts_with?(&1, "error"))
|> Enum.to_list()
```

Avoid Eager Evaluation:

Replace eager enumeration functions (Enum.map/2, Enum.filter/2) with their lazy counterparts (Stream.map/2, Stream.filter/2) when possible.

Example:

```elixir
Copy code
stream = Stream.map(1..10_000_000, &(&1 * 2))
```

Enum.take(stream, 5)  # Processes only the first 5 elements.

Leverage Infinite Streams:

Use streams like Stream.iterate/2 for generating sequences without defining bounds. This avoids creating large collections upfront.

Example:

```elixir
Copy code
Stream.iterate(1, &(&1 + 1))
|> Enum.take(10)  # [1, 2, 3, 4, 5, 6, 7, 8, 9, 10]
```

Efficient File and I/O Processing:

Stream data from files or other I/O sources to handle large inputs efficiently.

Example:

```elixir
Copy code
File.stream!("log.txt")
```

```elixir
|> Stream.filter(&String.contains?(&1, "critical"))
|> Enum.take(5)
```

Minimize Intermediate Results:

Streams avoid creating intermediate lists for each operation, saving both time and memory.

Performance Comparison: Enum vs. Stream

| Operation | Enum (Eager) | Stream (Lazy) |
| --- | --- | --- |
| Data Loading | Entire collection is loaded. | Data is processed incrementally. |
| Memory Usage | High (depends on dataset size). | Low (only processes required data). |
| Speed | Slower for large datasets. | Faster for selective operations. |

Example:

elixir
Copy code
```elixir
# Eager Evaluation
Enum.map(1..10_000, &(&1 * 2)) |> Enum.take(5)
```

```
# Lazy Evaluation
Stream.map(1..10_000, &(&1 * 2)) |> Enum.take(5)  #
Faster and memory-efficient
```

Scenarios Where Streams Shine

Log File Analysis:

Use streams to process large log files line by line, filtering for specific patterns.

Batch Processing:
.

Process chunks of data from an external API without preloading everything.

Real-Time Data Processing:

Handle live data streams with minimal delay and low memory consumption.

Pipeline Compositions:

Build complex data transformations with a series of lazy stream operations.

Tips for Effective Stream Usage

Consume Streams Judiciously: Always include a terminal function (e.g., Enum.to_list/1, Enum.take/2) to trigger computation.

Avoid Over-Chaining: Excessive chained operations can introduce overhead, so design pipelines carefully.
Profile Your Code: Use tools like :observer or benchmarking libraries to measure performance gains.

Conclusion

Streams are an essential feature in Elixir for optimizing performance. By employing lazy evaluation, incremental processing, and memory-efficient operations, streams enable developers to build scalable and performant applications while handling data-intensive tasks with ease.

## Chapter 11
## Domain-Specific Languages (DSLs) in Elixir

Domain-Specific Languages (DSLs) in Elixir are specialized mini-languages designed to simplify tasks within a particular domain, such as web routing, database queries, or configuration management. Elixir's clean syntax and powerful macro system make it an excellent choice for creating expressive and intuitive DSLs.

Key Features of DSLs in Elixir

Readability: Simplify domain-specific tasks with concise, human-readable syntax.

Reusability: Encapsulate complex logic into reusable constructs.

Integration: Combine DSLs with Elixir frameworks like Phoenix and Ecto for enhanced functionality.

## Example

A simple routing DSL:

```elixir
Copy code
defmodule MyRouter do
  defmacro route(method, path, action) do
    quote do
      IO.puts("Route: #{unquote(method)} #{unquote(path)} -> #{unquote(action)}")
    end
  end
end

import MyRouter

route :get, "/home", :home_page
route :post, "/submit", :submit_form
```

## Applications of DSLs

Web frameworks (e.g., Phoenix routing)
Database queries (e.g., Ecto queries)
Workflow automation and configuration

DSLs in Elixir improve code clarity and efficiency, making them essential tools for building scalable and maintainable applications.

## 11.1 What Are DSLs?

Domain-Specific Languages (DSLs) are specialized programming languages or constructs designed to address specific problems or tasks within a particular domain. Unlike general-purpose programming languages (e.g., Elixir, Python, Java), DSLs focus on providing an expressive, concise, and easy-to-use syntax tailored to the needs of their target domain.

Types of DSLs

Internal DSLs:

Built within a general-purpose programming language, leveraging its syntax and features.
Example: Elixir's Ecto query syntax.

External DSLs:

Developed as standalone languages with custom syntax and tools.
Example: SQL for database operations.

Key Characteristics of DSLs

Domain-Specific: Focused on solving problems in a specific area, such as web development, database queries, or configuration management.

Expressive Syntax: Designed to be easy to read and write, often resembling natural language or domain-specific concepts.

Abstracted Complexity: Hides low-level implementation details, allowing users to focus on the domain problem.

Examples of DSLs
SQL: Querying and managing relational databases.

HTML: Markup language for structuring web pages.

Ecto (Elixir): A DSL for building and running database queries.

elixir

Copy code

from p in Post, where: p.published == true

Benefits of DSLs

Simplifies Domain-Specific Tasks: Provides intuitive ways to express complex operations.

Improves Productivity: Reduces the time required to write and understand code.

Enhances Code Readability: Creates more natural and domain-focused APIs.

Reusable Constructs: Encourages reusable and maintainable patterns for the target domain.

Use Cases

Web Development: Routing, middleware configuration, and template rendering.

Database Queries: Simplifying CRUD operations with expressive query builders.

Workflow Automation: Defining tasks and pipelines in domain-specific syntax.

DSLs enable developers to work more efficiently within specialized domains, bridging the gap between domain expertise and software implementation.

## 11.2 Building DSLs with Elixir

Elixir is an excellent language for building Domain-Specific Languages (DSLs) due to its powerful metaprogramming capabilities, clean syntax, and flexible macro system. By leveraging Elixir's features, developers can create expressive and concise DSLs that simplify complex tasks within specific domains.

Why Build DSLs in Elixir?

Metaprogramming Capabilities: Elixir's macro system allows for the generation and manipulation of code at compile-time, making it ideal for creating DSLs.

Concise Syntax: Elixir's syntax is minimalistic and highly readable, making it easy to design domain-specific constructs that are both intuitive and powerful.

Immutability and Concurrency: These features of Elixir make it a robust language for building fault-tolerant, scalable systems, which can benefit DSLs used in distributed systems or parallel computing.

Key Concepts for Building DSLs in Elixir

Macros: Macros are the heart of Elixir's metaprogramming. They allow developers to write code that generates other code. By defining macros, you can create a clean, intuitive DSL for your domain.

Example of a simple macro:

elixir
Copy code

```elixir
defmodule MyDSL do
  defmacro greet(name) do
    quote do
      IO.puts("Hello, #{unquote(name)}!")
    end
  end
end
```

This macro would allow you to use greet("John"), which would print "Hello, John!".

Blocks and Pipelines: Elixir's ability to handle blocks and pipeline operators (|>) can make DSL syntax more fluid and readable. For example, you can design a query DSL using pipelines to represent data flow:

elixir
Copy code
```elixir
defmodule QueryDSL do
  defmacro filter(query, condition) do
    quote do
      Enum.filter(unquote(query), fn item -> unquote(condition) end)
    end
  end
end
```

Quote and Unquote: In Elixir, quote is used to capture code as data (AST), and unquote is used to inject values into that code. This is essential for building dynamic and flexible DSLs.

Example:

```elixir
Copy code
defmodule MyDSL do
  defmacro add(x, y) do
    quote do
      unquote(x) + unquote(y)
    end
  end
end
```

Steps for Building a DSL in Elixir

Define the Domain:

Clearly define the problem domain for which you are building the DSL. Understand the common tasks and behaviors you want to simplify for users.

Create the Macro(s):

Use macros to define the domain-specific syntax. Macros should encapsulate the logic or operations that users of your DSL will use, translating them into executable Elixir code.

Design the Syntax:

Design a clean, readable syntax that hides complexity and makes the DSL user-friendly. The goal is to make the DSL as close to natural language or domain-specific terms as possible.

Test and Iterate:

Continuously test the DSL with real-world scenarios. Ensure that it is both intuitive and powerful, adjusting the syntax as needed.

Example: Simple DSL for Defining Routes

Here's an example of a simple routing DSL to define HTTP routes, similar to what you might find in a web framework like Phoenix:

elixir
Copy code
```elixir
defmodule RouterDSL do
  defmacro route(method, path, action) do
    quote do
      IO.puts("Route: #{unquote(method)} #{unquote(path)} -> #{unquote(action)}")
    end
  end
end

# Using the DSL
import RouterDSL

route :get, "/home", :home_page
route :post, "/submit", :submit_form
```
This code would output:

vbnet
Copy code
```vbnet
Route: get /home -> home_page
Route: post /submit -> submit_form
```

Best Practices for Building DSLs

Keep It Simple:

Avoid overcomplicating the DSL. It should simplify the domain task, not add unnecessary complexity.

Make It Readable:

The DSL should be intuitive and readable, especially for developers who may not be familiar with the underlying Elixir syntax.

Hide Complexity:

The DSL should abstract away the complex logic or implementation details. Users of the DSL should focus only on the high-level domain-specific tasks.

Reuse Elixir's Conventions:

Where possible, try to align your DSL with Elixir's existing syntax and conventions to make it feel familiar to other Elixir developers.

Advanced Techniques for DSLs

Nested DSLs:

You can design DSLs that support nested structures for more complex tasks, such as configuration files or pipeline-based systems.

Integration with Elixir Libraries:

DSLs can be designed to integrate seamlessly with popular Elixir libraries like Phoenix or Ecto, making them more powerful and flexible in real-world applications.

Applications of DSLs in Elixir

Web Frameworks:

Elixir's Phoenix framework uses DSLs for defining routes, controllers, and views, making it easy to build web applications.

Database Queries:

Ecto provides a DSL for building complex database queries, making it simpler to interact with databases in an idiomatic Elixir way.

Configuration Management:

DSLs can help define configuration options for systems, allowing for more natural setups.

Task Scheduling and Pipelines:

Elixir's concurrency model, combined with DSLs, can help define and manage complex task schedules or data pipelines.

Conclusion

Building DSLs with Elixir allows developers to create highly expressive, readable, and domain-specific languages that simplify complex tasks. With Elixir's powerful metaprogramming capabilities and concise syntax, building a DSL becomes a seamless process, enabling developers to create efficient, maintainable, and intuitive systems tailored to specific needs.

11.3 Examples of DSLs in Action

Domain-Specific Languages (DSLs) have been used extensively in various programming environments to simplify complex tasks, making them more intuitive, readable, and efficient. Below are some notable examples of DSLs in action, both within Elixir and in other contexts, illustrating how DSLs can improve productivity, readability, and maintainability.

1. Phoenix Router DSL (Elixir)

In Elixir, Phoenix, a popular web framework, uses a DSL to define routes. The Phoenix routing DSL allows developers to map HTTP requests to controller actions in a clean and declarative way.

Example:

elixir
Copy code

```
defmodule MyAppWeb.Router do
  use MyAppWeb, :router

  # Define a GET route
  get "/home", HomeController, :index

  # Define a POST route
  post "/submit", SubmitController, :create
end
```

Here, get and post are part of the Phoenix DSL, which makes defining HTTP routes straightforward. This eliminates the need to manually configure lower-level HTTP logic, offering a high-level abstraction that developers can easily understand and maintain.

2. Ecto Query DSL (Elixir)

Elixir's Ecto library, which provides a query and database interaction DSL, allows developers to write database queries in a natural, readable way without having to write raw SQL.

Example:

elixir

Copy code

```
from u in User, where: u.age > 18, select: u.name
```

.

This query uses Elixir syntax to construct a query for retrieving the names of all users over the age of 18. The query is declarative, focusing on the intent (retrieving user names) rather than the underlying SQL mechanics.

Ecto abstracts away SQL complexities and gives developers a DSL that closely aligns with Elixir's functional programming style, improving both expressiveness and maintainability.

3. ExUnit Test DSL (Elixir)

Elixir's built-in testing framework, ExUnit, provides a DSL for defining and running tests. The DSL helps structure test cases in a clear, readable way and integrates seamlessly with Elixir's overall syntax.

Example:

elixir

```
Copy code
defmodule MyAppTest do
  use ExUnit.Case

  test "addition of two numbers" do
    assert 1 + 1 == 2
  end
end
```

The test macro in ExUnit is part of the DSL, making the test structure highly readable and closely tied to the natural language of the test description. This structure allows for easy identification of test cases and expected results.

4. SQL (External DSL)

SQL (Structured Query Language) is a classic example of an external DSL. It provides a specialized syntax for querying and manipulating databases, optimized for data retrieval and management.

Example:

sql
Copy code

SELECT name, age FROM users WHERE age > 18;
SQL allows users to interact with databases in a domain-specific way, abstracting the complexities of low-level database operations into a simple, declarative syntax.

5. HTML (External DSL)

HTML (Hypertext Markup Language) is another example of an external DSL. It is designed specifically for defining the structure and content of web pages, offering a markup system tailored to web development.

Example:

```html
Copy code
<!DOCTYPE html>
<html>
 <head>
  <title>My Page</title>
 </head>
 <body>
  <h1>Welcome to My Website</h1>
  <p>This is a paragraph.</p>
```

```
</body>
</html>
```

HTML uses tags to define the structure of a page, such as headers, paragraphs, and links. Its syntax is simple and specialized for web content, making it an ideal example of an external DSL.

6. CSS (External DSL)

CSS (Cascading Style Sheets) is another external DSL used for defining the visual presentation of web pages. It is highly specialized for styling HTML elements and offers a concise, readable syntax for designers and developers.

Example:

```css
Copy code
body {
  font-family: Arial, sans-serif;
  background-color: #f0f0f0;
}
```

CSS is a declarative language that abstracts the complex styling logic of web development, allowing developers to focus on designing layouts, colors, and fonts in a simplified manner.

7. Regular Expressions (External DSL)

Regular expressions (regex) are another type of DSL that allow developers to define search patterns for text processing. While regex syntax is specialized and cryptic, it is incredibly powerful for tasks like validation, search, and text transformation.

Example:

```regex
Copy code
^\d{3}-\d{2}-\d{4}$
```

This regex pattern matches Social Security numbers in the format XXX-XX-XXXX. Regular expressions provide a domain-specific way of handling text pattern matching, reducing the need to write complex string manipulation code.

8. Rake (Ruby DSL)

Rake is a build automation tool for Ruby that uses a domain-specific language to define tasks and dependencies. It's commonly used in Ruby on Rails for running tasks like database migrations, tests, and other utilities.

Example:

```ruby
Copy code
task :default => [:environment, :test]

task :test do
  puts "Running tests..."
end
```

Rake allows developers to define tasks in a concise and domain-specific way, making it easy to automate and manage various operations within a Ruby application.

9. CSS Grid and Flexbox (Web Design DSLs)

CSS Grid and Flexbox are specialized DSLs within CSS that focus on defining layouts.

These CSS layout techniques provide declarative syntax for arranging elements on a page in complex, responsive grids or flexible layouts.

Example:

```css
Copy code
.container {
  display: grid;
  grid-template-columns: repeat(3, 1fr);
}
```

CSS Grid allows for defining grid-based layouts, making complex layouts more manageable without resorting to hacks or manual positioning.

Conclusion

DSLs are powerful tools for developers that enable them to work more efficiently in specific domains. Whether built within a general-purpose programming language like Elixir or external to it like SQL or HTML, DSLs offer domain-specific syntax that simplifies complex tasks and improves code readability. By abstracting away unnecessary complexity, DSLs enable developers to focus on high-level logic, leading to more maintainable and expressive codebases.

# PART V: BUILDING APPLICATIONS WITH ELIXIR

## Chapter 12.
## Web Development with Phoenix Framework

Phoenix is a powerful, full-stack web development framework written in Elixir, designed to make building reliable, scalable, and fast web applications easier. It leverages Elixir's strengths, such as concurrency and fault tolerance, to provide high-performance, real-time capabilities, making it ideal for modern web applications.

Key Features of Phoenix:

Real-Time Features with Channels: Phoenix includes built-in support for real-time features using Channels. This allows for seamless communication between the client and server through websockets, making it ideal for applications that require live updates (e.g., chat apps, real-time notifications, live feeds).

Built-in Web Server (Cowboy): Phoenix comes with Cowboy, a high-performance HTTP server optimized for handling a large number of simultaneous connections, which is critical for real-time web apps.

MVC Architecture: Phoenix follows the Model-View-Controller (MVC) pattern, separating the application into distinct layers (models, views, and controllers). This structure promotes maintainability and scalability.

Ecto for Database Interactions: Phoenix integrates with Ecto, an Elixir library for working with databases, making database queries more intuitive and easy to manage, with support for migrations, validations, and query building.

Routing and URL Generation: Phoenix offers a declarative approach to routing, enabling developers to map URLs to controller actions with ease, ensuring clean and readable routing definitions.

Static Asset Management: Phoenix provides built-in support for managing static assets like CSS, JavaScript, and images, with features for optimizing and compiling them for production environments.

Benefits of Using Phoenix:

Scalability: Phoenix leverages Elixir's actor model and lightweight processes, which makes it exceptionally scalable, capable of handling large numbers of concurrent users without sacrificing performance.

Fault Tolerance: Phoenix inherits Elixir's fault-tolerant design, ensuring that web applications can remain responsive even under failure conditions.

Speed: Thanks to Elixir's lightweight processes and Phoenix's optimized architecture, applications built with Phoenix can handle real-time, high-traffic loads with minimal latency.

Developer Productivity: Phoenix offers an intuitive and developer-friendly environment with tools like code reloading, a built-in web server, and a powerful templating engine (EEx).

Overall, Phoenix is an excellent choice for web development, especially when building real-time, scalable, and resilient applications. It combines the speed and scalability of Elixir with modern web development patterns and tools, making it a compelling option for both beginner and experienced developers.

12.1 Overview of Phoenix Framework

Phoenix is a robust and highly performant web framework built on Elixir, designed for building scalable and fault-tolerant web applications. It leverages the concurrency and reliability of Elixir and its underlying Erlang virtual machine (BEAM) to deliver real-time web applications with ease. Phoenix is known for its speed, scalability, and ability to handle concurrent connections efficiently, making it ideal for building highly interactive applications, such as chat systems, notifications, and real-time feeds.

Key Components of Phoenix Framework:

MVC Architecture (Model-View-Controller): Phoenix follows the traditional Model-View-Controller (MVC) architecture, providing a clean separation of concerns that promotes maintainability and scalability.

Model: Handles data and database interactions through Ecto, which simplifies querying and working with databases. View: Responsible for rendering templates and generating the response for the user.

Controller: Manages the flow of data between the model and view, responding to user requests.

Real-Time Communication with Channels: One of the standout features of Phoenix is its built-in support for real-time communication through Channels. Channels allow bidirectional communication between clients and the server using WebSockets, enabling real-time features like chat rooms, live updates, and notifications without constant HTTP requests.

Routing: Phoenix has an expressive and declarative routing system. Developers define routes in the router.ex file, where they map incoming requests to controller actions. This makes routing both easy to manage and understand.

Ecto for Database Interactions: Phoenix integrates seamlessly with Ecto, an Elixir library for working with databases. Ecto provides an elegant interface for querying, defining schemas, managing database migrations, and performing other database-related tasks, all while maintaining the power and flexibility of Elixir.

Static Asset Management: Phoenix comes with built-in support for handling static assets (CSS, JavaScript, images) through tools like Webpack and asset pipeline integrations. This ensures that applications are optimized for production with minimized and compressed asset files.

Built-in Web Server (Cowboy): Phoenix uses the Cowboy HTTP server by default. Cowboy is a lightweight, high-performance HTTP server designed to handle many concurrent connections, making it ideal for real-time applications that require low-latency responses and large-scale support.

Templating Engine (EEx): Phoenix uses EEx (Embedded Elixir), a templating engine that allows you to embed Elixir code within HTML. This allows dynamic rendering of content, offering powerful, flexible templates while maintaining a clear separation of concerns between logic and presentation.

Benefits of Using Phoenix:

Concurrency and Scalability: Phoenix takes full advantage of Elixir's actor model, where lightweight processes (called "actors") handle each connection. This allows Phoenix to handle thousands (or even millions) of concurrent users without significant performance degradation.

Fault Tolerance: Phoenix inherits Elixir's fault-tolerant design, ensuring that failures within the system can be isolated and handled without crashing the entire application. This is crucial for building resilient systems that need to stay operational even during errors or hardware failures.

Real-Time Support: Phoenix simplifies the process of building real-time applications with its built-in Channels feature. Whether you're building a chat app, a live dashboard, or an online game, Phoenix enables seamless real-time communication between the server and clients.

Developer Productivity: Phoenix comes with several built-in tools, such as code reloading, powerful generators, and detailed error messages, which make development faster and more efficient. The framework encourages writing clean, modular code, improving both productivity and maintainability.

High Performance: Thanks to the concurrency model of Elixir and the efficiency of the BEAM, Phoenix is designed to handle high levels of traffic while maintaining low latency and responsiveness.

Phoenix Ecosystem and Tools:

Phoenix LiveView: Phoenix LiveView is an extension of the Phoenix framework that allows developers to build interactive, real-time user interfaces with minimal JavaScript. By leveraging WebSockets, LiveView enables dynamic, live updates to the UI without needing to reload the page or write complex JavaScript.

Phoenix Contexts: Phoenix introduces the concept of "contexts" to group related functionality, making it easier to manage and organize business logic. This approach leads to a more modular and scalable codebase.

Phoenix PubSub: The PubSub (Publish-Subscribe) system in Phoenix allows different parts of an application to communicate with each other efficiently. It's commonly used for broadcasting messages in real-time applications, such as sending notifications to all connected users.

Phoenix Presence: Phoenix Presence is a library used to track user presence in real time. It's commonly used in applications like chat rooms or collaborative tools to show who is online and track user activity.

Conclusion:

Phoenix is an excellent choice for developers looking to build modern, high-performance, and scalable web applications. It combines the reliability and concurrency of Elixir with a rich set of web development tools and real-time features, making it perfect for building everything from simple websites to complex, real-time applications. With its focus on developer productivity, scalability, and fault tolerance, Phoenix provides an elegant and powerful framework for building robust web applications.

## 12.2 Building a Simple Web Application

Building a simple web application with Phoenix is an excellent way to get started with Elixir's powerful web framework. Phoenix offers a full-stack solution, including routing, templates, controllers, and a seamless connection to databases. Below is a step-by-step guide to creating a basic web application that displays a list of items.

Step 1: Setting Up the Project
To get started, you need to have Elixir and Phoenix installed. If you haven't done this yet, follow these steps:

Install Elixir: If you haven't installed Elixir, you can download it from here.

Install Phoenix: After installing Elixir, you can install Phoenix by running:

bash
Copy code

mix archive.install hex phx_new

Create a New Phoenix Project: Create a new Phoenix project with the following command:

```bash
Copy code
mix phx.new my_app
```

This command will create a new Phoenix project in the my_app folder with all the necessary dependencies and configuration files. Follow the prompts to install the dependencies.

Navigate to Your Project Directory:

```bash
Copy code
cd my_app
```
Start the Phoenix Server: You can start the Phoenix server by running:

```bash
Copy code
```

mix phx.server

Open your browser and go to http://localhost:4000, where you will see the default Phoenix welcome page.

Step 2: Creating a Simple Resource

In this step, we'll create a simple resource called "Item" to store and display a list of items.

Generate the Item Resource: Phoenix comes with generators that create the necessary files for resources like controllers, views, and templates. To generate an "Item" resource with a name and description, run:

```bash
Copy code
mix phx.gen.html Items Item name:string description:text
```

This will generate several files:

A migration for the database.
A controller for handling requests.
Views for rendering HTML.
Templates for displaying the items.

Run the Migration: To create the items table in the database, run the migration:

```bash
Copy code
mix ecto.migrate
```

Step 3: Define Routes

Phoenix uses a router to define the paths for accessing various resources. The router.ex file contains the routes for the application.

Add the Resource Route: Open lib/my_app_web/router.ex and ensure the following route exists:

```elixir
Copy code
scope "/", MyAppWeb do
  pipe_through :browser


  resources "/items", ItemController
end
```

This tells Phoenix to generate routes for the ItemController, including index, show, new, and edit routes.

Step 4: Create a Controller

The ItemController handles the requests for the item resource.

Add the Controller Logic: Open lib/my_app_web/controllers/item_controller.ex and add the following code:

elixir
Copy code
```elixir
defmodule MyAppWeb.ItemController do
  use MyAppWeb, :controller

  alias MyApp.Items
  alias MyApp.Items.Item

  def index(conn, _params) do
    items = Items.list_items()
    render(conn, "index.html", items: items)
  end

  def new(conn, _params) do
    changeset = Items.change_item(%Item{})
    render(conn, "new.html", changeset: changeset)
```

```
end

def create(conn, %{"item" => item_params}) do
  case Items.create_item(item_params) do
    {:ok, item} ->
      conn
      |> put_flash(:info, "Item created successfully.")
      |> redirect(to: Routes.item_path(conn, :show, item))

    {:error, %Ecto.Changeset{} = changeset} ->
      render(conn, "new.html", changeset: changeset)
  end
end
end
```

This controller includes:

The index action to list all items.
The new and create actions for adding new items.

Step 5: Create Views and Templates

Next, you need to create the views and templates for displaying the items.

Create the Item View: Open lib/my_app_web/views/item_view.ex and add:

elixir
Copy code
```
defmodule MyAppWeb.ItemView do
  use MyAppWeb, :view
end
```

Create the Templates: In the lib/my_app_web/templates/item directory, you will need to create the following files:

index.html.eex for listing the items.
new.html.eex for the form to add new items.

Example of index.html.eex:

html
Copy code
```
<h1>Items</h1>
<%= for item <- @items do %>
  <p><%= item.name %> - <%= item.description %></p>
<% end %>
```

Example of new.html.eex:

html
Copy code

```
<h1>New Item</h1>
<%= form_for @changeset, Routes.item_path(@conn,
:create), fn f -> %>
  <%= text_input f, :name %>
  <%= text_input f, :description %>
  <%= submit "Create Item" %>
<% end %>
```

Step 6: Test the Application

After completing the above steps, your web application should be up and running. You can now:

Visit http://localhost:4000/items to view the list of items.
Go to http://localhost:4000/items/new to add new items using the form.

Phoenix automatically handles the routes, controllers, and views for the items, allowing you to focus on building the application's business logic.

## Conclusion

In this tutorial, you've learned how to build a simple web application using Phoenix. By generating a basic resource, defining routes, and creating controllers and views, you now have the foundation for a fully functional web app. Phoenix's simplicity, combined with Elixir's performance and concurrency features, makes it an excellent choice for building scalable, maintainable web applications.

## 12.3 Functional Programming in Web Development

Functional programming (FP) is a programming paradigm that emphasizes immutability, first-class functions, and pure functions. While it's traditionally more associated with back-end development, FP can also be incredibly effective in web development. By leveraging the principles of functional programming, web developers can create more predictable, maintainable, and scalable applications.

## Core Concepts of Functional Programming

Immutability: In functional programming, once a value is created, it cannot be changed. Instead of modifying data, new data is created from existing values. This helps prevent side effects, making programs easier to reason about.

Pure Functions: Functions are considered pure if their output depends solely on their input, with no side effects. This leads to more predictable behavior, making the code easier to test and maintain.

First-Class Functions: Functions in FP are treated as first-class citizens, meaning they can be passed as arguments, returned as values, and assigned to variables. This enables higher-order functions, which can take other functions as inputs or outputs, creating more abstract and reusable code.

Declarative Programming: Functional programming focuses on "what" should be done rather than "how." This declarative nature can simplify the code by abstracting away lower-level implementation details.

Benefits of Functional Programming in Web Development

Better Code Readability and Maintainability: Because functional programming emphasizes immutability and pure functions, code is often more predictable and easier to understand. There are fewer unexpected changes to state, which makes it easier to follow the logic flow.

Concurrency and Parallelism: Web applications often need to handle multiple tasks simultaneously, such as handling multiple user requests or interacting with a database. Functional programming languages, like Elixir or JavaScript (with promises and async/await), offer built-in support for concurrency and parallelism. Immutable data structures ensure that multiple processes can work on data simultaneously without fear of corrupting the state.

Testability: Pure functions have no side effects and always produce the same output for the same input, making them highly testable. This is crucial in web development where reliability is key. By writing small, composable functions, developers can write unit tests for individual components more easily.

State Management: In web applications, managing state can often become complex. By using immutable data structures and leveraging pure functions, state management becomes simpler and more predictable. This is especially important in single-page applications (SPAs) where managing client-side state is a critical concern.

Functional Programming in Web Frameworks

Functional programming can be leveraged across various parts of web development, including front-end, back-end, and even the database layer.

Back-End (Elixir/Phoenix):

Elixir, a functional language, is known for its high scalability and concurrency features. The Phoenix framework, built with Elixir, uses functional programming concepts to build reliable and scalable web applications.

Functional programming enables developers to easily scale their applications, handle thousands of simultaneous requests, and build fault-tolerant systems. Phoenix's routing and controller layers make use of pure functions and immutable data, enabling developers to handle concurrent connections efficiently.

Front-End (JavaScript/React):

JavaScript, while not strictly a functional language, supports functional programming features. Libraries like React embrace functional principles such as immutability and pure functions.

In React, components are often implemented as pure functions, and state management tools like Redux encourage immutability, making state predictable and easier to debug.

With the advent of hooks and higher-order functions, React's functional style allows developers to break down complex logic into simpler, more reusable pieces.

Database Layer:

Functional programming can also be used effectively in the database layer of web applications. In functional programming, queries can be treated as immutable data structures, and operations on those queries are purely functional.

Functional databases like Datomic focus on immutability, providing a way to store data in a consistent state without worrying about transactional inconsistencies.

Functional Programming in Modern Web Development

Modern web development benefits greatly from the functional paradigm. With the rise of single-page applications (SPAs), real-time communication, and microservices, FP helps maintain clean, scalable, and reliable code.

Let's explore some specific use cases:

Handling Asynchronous Operations: Web development often involves asynchronous tasks such as HTTP requests, real-time data updates, or background jobs. Functional programming makes managing these operations more straightforward by treating them as values that can be manipulated using first-class functions. In JavaScript, promises and async/await patterns make asynchronous operations more intuitive and manageable.

Serverless Architectures: Functional programming fits naturally into serverless architectures, where statelessness and immutability are key. Functions in serverless environments are often designed to be stateless, and the functional approach lends itself well to this architecture. Serverless platforms, like AWS Lambda or Google Cloud Functions, allow developers to build modular, scalable, and resilient web applications based on functional programming principles.

Reactive Programming: Reactive programming is a programming paradigm focused on asynchronous data streams. It's particularly useful for building applications with real-time features such as chat applications, live feeds, and stock market tracking. Functional programming integrates well with reactive programming, especially with frameworks like RxJS (for JavaScript), which uses streams and operators that allow for cleaner, declarative code.

Challenges of Functional Programming in Web Development

Learning Curve: For developers new to functional programming, there can be a steep learning curve. Understanding the core principles, such as immutability, higher-order functions, and pure functions, may require a shift in thinking compared to traditional object-oriented programming.

Tooling and Libraries: While the functional programming ecosystem is growing, it may not always have as many resources or libraries as more traditional web development paradigms. Developers may need to create custom solutions or adapt existing tools to their needs.

Performance Overhead: In some cases, functional programming's emphasis on immutability and creating new objects rather than modifying existing ones can lead to performance overhead. However, with careful optimization and the right language (e.g., Elixir or JavaScript), this overhead can be minimized.

Conclusion

Functional programming is a powerful paradigm that brings significant advantages to web development. Its principles of immutability, pure functions, and first-class functions can help developers build more predictable, maintainable, and scalable applications. Whether building with Elixir and Phoenix on the back end, or JavaScript and React on the front end, functional programming offers a compelling approach for modern web applications that require high concurrency, state management, and real-time updates. By embracing FP, developers can create cleaner code, reduce bugs, and ultimately improve the robustness of their web applications.

# Chapter 13
## Testing and Debugging Functional Code

Testing and debugging are essential practices in ensuring the reliability and correctness of any software. In functional programming, these tasks are slightly different from traditional object-oriented approaches due to the emphasis on immutability, pure functions, and declarative code.

Testing Functional Code

Unit Testing:

Pure Functions: Testing pure functions in functional programming is easier because they have no side effects and always return the same output for the same input. This makes unit tests predictable and reliable.

Property-Based Testing: This testing strategy focuses on testing the properties of functions (e.g., commutativity, associativity) rather than specific inputs and outputs. Tools like ExUnit in Elixir or QuickCheck in Haskell are often used for property-based testing.

Mocking:

While mocking is less common in functional programming due to the reliance on pure functions, it can still be used in scenarios where interacting with external systems is necessary. However, you should avoid excessive reliance on mocks to preserve the purity of your tests.

Test-Driven Development (TDD):

Functional programming lends itself well to TDD, as the focus is on writing small, pure functions that are easy to test. TDD encourages writing tests before code, and the simplicity and immutability of functional code make this process smooth and effective.

Integration and System Testing:

Since functional code tends to be more modular, integration tests become straightforward by composing smaller functions. These tests can focus on how well the components work together, especially in handling external states like databases or APIs.

Debugging Functional Code

Immutability:

Debugging functional code can be easier because the state doesn't change unexpectedly. If a bug arises, it's often due to the function's logic rather than side effects or changing state, making it easier to trace.

Pure Functions and Traceability:

With pure functions, inputs and outputs are always consistent, so it's easier to isolate bugs. When testing or debugging, you can focus on the function itself without worrying about external state or dependencies.

Error Handling:

Elixir, for instance, has built-in support for error handling through supervision trees and let-let mechanisms. In functional languages like Elixir, errors can be modeled as values, which makes error handling and debugging clearer and more declarative.

Functional Debugging Tools:

Languages like Elixir provide tools like the Interactive Elixir (IEx) shell, which allows developers to interactively test functions, experiment with code, and quickly diagnose issues. The use of immutable data structures can make the debugging process more straightforward since you can be confident that no data is being altered unexpectedly.

Conclusion

Testing and debugging functional code is streamlined by the core principles of functional programming, such as immutability and pure functions. These features reduce side effects and make the code more predictable, making testing easier and debugging more efficient. With the right tools and techniques, functional code can be both easier to test and more reliable to debug, resulting in robust and maintainable software.

## 13.1 Writing Tests for Functional Applications

Testing is a vital part of software development, ensuring that applications work as expected and are free from defects. Writing tests for functional applications, which emphasize immutability, pure functions, and declarative code, offers unique advantages. Functional programming paradigms simplify testing by making code more predictable and modular. However, writing tests for functional applications still requires following best practices and understanding how functional concepts interact with the testing process.

Types of Tests for Functional Applications
Unit Tests:

Definition: Unit tests verify individual functions or units of code in isolation.
Testing Pure Functions: One of the key advantages of functional programming is the simplicity of testing pure functions. Since pure functions always return the same result for the same input and have no side effects, they are inherently testable. Unit tests can directly check the

function's input and output without concerns about external dependencies or mutable state.

Example in Elixir:
elixir
Copy code
```
defmodule MathTest do
  use ExUnit.Case
  test "adding two numbers" do
    assert Math.add(1, 2) == 3
  end
end
```

Property-Based Tests:

Definition: Property-based testing involves verifying that certain properties hold for a function or system, rather than testing with specific inputs and outputs.

Functional Focus: Since functional programming often emphasizes general functions that operate on various types of data, property-based testing is a natural fit. In languages like Elixir or Haskell, you can use property-based testing libraries like ExUnit (Elixir) or QuickCheck (Haskell) to validate general properties of functions.

Example in Elixir:

elixir

Copy code

```elixir
defmodule MathTest do
  use ExUnit.Case
  use ExUnitProperties

  property "addition is commutative" do
    forall a <- integer(), b <- integer() do
      assert Math.add(a, b) == Math.add(b, a)
    end
  end
end
```

Integration Tests:

Definition: Integration tests check if different parts of the application work together as expected. These tests usually involve multiple functions or modules that interact with one another.

Testing External Systems: In functional applications, integration tests may involve interacting with external systems like databases or APIs. Since functional programming often encourages immutability and statelessness, integrating external systems is usually done through well-defined interfaces or through dependency injection.

Example: Testing how a module interacts with a database or external API by verifying the end-to-end process.

Acceptance Tests:

Definition: Acceptance tests check whether the entire system meets the specified requirements or use cases. These tests are typically higher-level tests that simulate the behavior of the application from an end-user's perspective.
Example: A web application built using the Phoenix framework could have acceptance tests verifying that user inputs in forms result in the correct updates to the database.

Best Practices for Writing Tests in Functional Applications

Test Small, Independent Functions:

Functional programming promotes small, composable functions that do one thing well. These functions are often easier to test, as their behavior is deterministic (i.e., the same inputs will always produce the same outputs). Focus on testing individual functions first and ensure they work in isolation before testing larger modules.

Leverage Immutability:

In functional applications, data is immutable, which means once a piece of data is created, it cannot be changed. This leads to more predictable code and simplifies tests. Avoiding mutable state ensures that tests will not interfere with each other and that tests for one function will not unintentionally break others.

Write Tests Before Code (TDD):

Test-Driven Development (TDD) can be particularly useful in functional programming. The declarative nature of functional code makes it easy to write tests first. By writing tests for the expected behavior of functions, developers ensure that their code satisfies the desired properties from the outset.

Test for Edge Cases:

Although functional applications often have predictable behavior, edge cases and boundaries should still be tested. For instance, in recursive functions, test cases should include empty input, null values, or very large inputs to ensure the function behaves as expected in extreme scenarios.

Use Mocking and Stubbing Wisely:

In functional programming, the reliance on pure functions reduces the need for mocking or stubbing dependencies. However, when integrating with external systems, tools like Mox in Elixir can be used to mock certain behaviors for the purpose of testing.

Ensure High Code Coverage:

Given the modularity of functional applications, ensure that your tests cover all branches of the code, including any recursive functions, error handling, or exception cases. Tools like ExCoveralls in Elixir can help measure test coverage and ensure that all aspects of the codebase are adequately tested. Tools for Testing Functional Applications

ExUnit (Elixir):

ExUnit is the default testing framework for Elixir. It allows developers to write unit, integration, and property-based tests for Elixir applications. ExUnit supports asynchronous tests, allowing tests to run in parallel, which is particularly useful in concurrent Elixir applications.

QuickCheck (Haskell):

QuickCheck is a property-based testing library for Haskell. It can automatically generate random test data and check whether the properties hold for that data, making it easier to find edge cases and unexpected bugs in your functions.

Jest (JavaScript):

While JavaScript is not purely functional, libraries like Jest can be used to write tests for functional applications in JavaScript, especially with frameworks like React or Redux. Jest supports features like snapshot testing, which can be useful when testing immutable data structures.

Conclusion

Writing tests for functional applications has significant advantages, such as higher predictability, easier test maintenance, and better separation of concerns. By leveraging the power of pure functions, immutability, and modularity, functional code tends to be more testable and maintainable than code written in other paradigms. Tools and frameworks like ExUnit, QuickCheck, and Jest make it easier to write unit tests, property-based tests, and integration tests for functional applications. Following best practices like writing tests before code (TDD), testing small, independent functions, and ensuring high code coverage will help create more reliable and robust functional applications.

## 13.2 Debugging Elixir Applications

Debugging is a critical process in software development, helping developers identify and fix issues within an application. Elixir, a functional language built on the Erlang virtual machine (BEAM), offers a number of tools and techniques that make debugging both efficient and effective. Given Elixir's emphasis on immutability, concurrency, and fault tolerance, debugging Elixir applications may differ from debugging in other programming languages.

Here's an overview of the key debugging approaches and tools for Elixir applications.

1. Interactive Elixir (IEx)

IEx is the interactive shell that comes with Elixir. It provides a powerful environment for evaluating expressions, testing functions, and inspecting code behavior interactively, which is especially useful for debugging.

Testing Code in IEx: You can quickly test parts of your code in IEx to see how they behave without having to run the entire application. This is particularly helpful when trying to isolate issues with specific functions or modules.

Inspecting Variables: You can inspect the state of variables, the values returned from functions, and any data structures by entering commands directly into the IEx shell. This allows you to explore how your code behaves at runtime.

Example:

elixir

Copy code

```
iex> my_function()
```

Real-Time Evaluation: Modify code in real time and immediately test the changes in IEx without the need for recompiling or restarting the application.

2. Debugging Tools in Elixir

Elixir provides a suite of built-in tools and libraries to make debugging more efficient. Some of the most useful tools include:

Logger:

Elixir's built-in Logger module is essential for tracking runtime events, errors, and warnings. By adding logging calls to your application, you can capture useful information about what the system is doing at different points.
Logging levels include :debug, :info, :warn, and :error. This allows you to control the verbosity of logs and focus on the relevant parts of your application.

Example:

elixir

Copy code

```
Logger.debug("This is a debug message")
Logger.error("An error occurred: #{inspect(error)}")
```

:observer:

Elixir provides an interactive tool called :observer for observing the internal state of an Elixir system. It allows you to visualize system processes, memory usage, and much more in a GUI interface.

This is especially useful when debugging issues related to concurrency, process states, and system resources.

elixir

Copy code

```
:observer.start()
```

IO.inspect/2:

The IO.inspect/2 function is a lightweight debugging tool that allows developers to print the value of variables or expressions directly to the console.

This is particularly helpful for inspecting complex data structures, like lists or maps, and understanding the flow of data through the system.

Example:

elixir
Copy code
IO.inspect(my_variable, label: "Inspecting my_variable")

3. Debugging Concurrency Issues

One of the primary strengths of Elixir is its concurrency model, based on the Actor Model and the BEAM VM. While concurrency allows for scalable and responsive systems, it also introduces unique challenges in debugging.

Process Monitoring:

Elixir's lightweight processes, managed by the BEAM, allow you to monitor and track their state, which is crucial when debugging concurrency issues.

You can monitor processes with Process.monitor/1 and use :sys.get_status/1 to inspect the status of a process.

Example:

```elixir
Copy code
Process.monitor(pid)
```

Tracing:

Elixir allows you to trace messages between processes and monitor their execution. You can use the :dbg module to attach traces to processes, observe function calls, and track messages being passed between them.

Example:

```elixir
Copy code
:dbg.tracer()
:dbg.p(:all, :call)
:dbg.tpl(ModuleName, :function_name, [])
```

Deadlocks and Race Conditions:

Concurrency-related issues like deadlocks or race conditions can be challenging to debug. Elixir's process isolation (each process has its own memory) reduces the chance of these problems, but they can still occur when processes depend on each other's state.

Careful use of timeouts, locks, and semantics of process messaging can help mitigate these issues.

4. Exception Handling and Stack Traces

When an error occurs in Elixir, the system generates stack traces that provide valuable insight into where the error occurred and which functions were involved. Elixir follows the "let it crash" philosophy, which means that processes are expected to crash in case of failure, and their errors should be handled via supervisors, but you can still catch and handle exceptions as needed.

Stack Traces:

Stack traces in Elixir provide detailed information about where errors happen in your code, including the module, function, and line number.

Elixir's error messages are generally clear and helpful, making it easier to trace issues back to specific parts of your code.

Example:

```elixir
Copy code
try do
  some_potentially_failing_function()
catch
    :error, reason -> Logger.error("An error occurred: #{reason}")
end
```

Supervisor Strategy:

In Elixir, supervisors are responsible for managing processes and handling failures. When debugging, ensure that you understand the strategy your application uses for fault tolerance. Common strategies include :one_for_one, :one_for_all, and

:rest_for_one.

If a process crashes unexpectedly, check the supervisor's logs to understand the reason behind the failure.

5. Remote Debugging and Monitoring

For production systems, debugging locally might not be feasible, and remote debugging becomes necessary. Elixir's distributed nature makes it easy to connect to remote nodes for debugging and monitoring.

Connecting to Remote Nodes:

Elixir allows you to connect to remote nodes using Node.connect/1. Once connected, you can use tools like IEx to interact with the remote system, inspect processes, and evaluate code remotely.

Example:

```elixir
Copy code
Node.connect(:remote_node@hostname)
```

Remote Tracing:

Elixir allows you to attach a debugger remotely using the :dbg module, so you can trace processes or debug live systems in production.

6. Profiling and Performance Debugging

Elixir also provides tools for performance debugging, which is crucial for identifying bottlenecks or inefficient code in concurrent systems.

:fprof:

The :fprof module is used for profiling function calls, helping you measure the execution time of specific functions.

Example:

```
elixir
Copy code
:fprof.profile(:start)
:fprof.profile(:stop)
:fprof.profile(:analyze)
:exprof:
```

An external library that offers more advanced profiling features for Elixir, including detailed function-level profiling and performance analysis.

Conclusion

Debugging Elixir applications is streamlined by a range of powerful tools and techniques that cater to both functional and concurrent programming paradigms. Using IEx for interactive testing, Logger for tracking runtime behavior, and tools like :observer for system-level monitoring, developers can quickly identify and resolve issues. Additionally, the actor model, process isolation, and fault-tolerant design of Elixir applications provide natural resiliency, which can make debugging more manageable. With a deep understanding of these debugging techniques and tools, Elixir developers can ensure their applications run smoothly and efficiently in both development and production environments.

13.3 Tools and Best Practices

Debugging is an essential aspect of software development that allows developers to identify and resolve issues in their code. In Elixir, debugging is made easier thanks to a variety of tools, techniques, and best practices that are specifically designed for the language's functional, concurrent, and fault-tolerant nature. Below are some of the most powerful tools available for Elixir developers, as well as best practices to follow for efficient debugging and troubleshooting.

1. Essential Debugging Tools in Elixir

.

Elixir provides a rich set of debugging tools that help developers understand their application's behavior and resolve issues faster. The following tools are some of the most commonly used:

IEx (Interactive Elixir)

What It Is: IEx is the interactive shell in Elixir, providing a real-time environment where you can evaluate expressions, test functions, and inspect code without the need for restarting the application.

How It Helps: By entering commands into the IEx shell, you can quickly experiment with your code, evaluate variables, and explore how different functions behave, all while the application is running. IEx helps developers diagnose problems directly in the runtime environment.

Example:

```
elixir
Copy code
iex> MyModule.my_function()
```

Logger

What It Is: The Logger module is Elixir's built-in logging tool, which is useful for tracking the flow of execution, capturing variable states, and recording errors and warnings.

How It Helps: By adding log statements at critical points in your code, you can gather insights about your application's behavior, track down issues, and monitor performance.

Example:

```elixir
Copy code
Logger.debug("Debugging message")
Logger.info("Application started")
Logger.error("An error occurred: #{inspect(error)}")
:observer
```

What It Is: :observer is a graphical tool that allows developers to inspect the internal state of an Elixir application, including process states, memory usage, and system performance.

How It Helps: The tool provides real-time information about processes, message queues, and system resource utilization, which is invaluable for understanding concurrency-related issues and monitoring live applications.

Example:

```elixir
Copy code
:observer.start()
```

IO.inspect/2

What It Is: A simple tool for inspecting the values of variables and expressions at runtime.

How It Helps: Developers can use

IO.inspect/2 to print out values of variables, data structures, and expressions to the console, helping to visualize the flow of data through the system.

Example:

```elixir
Copy code
IO.inspect(my_variable, label: "Inspecting my_variable")
```

2. Best Practices for Effective Debugging in Elixir

While Elixir offers powerful tools for debugging, it's equally important to adopt best practices that can streamline the debugging process and help identify issues more efficiently. Here are some best practices for debugging Elixir applications:

Use Descriptive Logging

Why It's Important: Log messages are crucial for tracking the behavior of an application, but they need to be descriptive and clear to be useful.

Best Practice: Make use of appropriate logging levels (e.g., :debug, :info, :warn, :error) to categorize the severity of messages. Include relevant context in log messages, such as function names, variable values, and error details.

Example:

```elixir
Copy code
Logger.info("Starting the process with parameters: #{inspect(params)}")
Logger.error("Failed to process data: #{inspect(error)}")
```

Test in Isolation Using IEx

Why It's Important: Debugging is easier when you isolate the part of the application where the problem occurs.

Best Practice: Use IEx to test isolated portions of your code and explore different functions independently. This can help you pinpoint issues more efficiently and prevent having to restart the entire application.

Monitor Processes

Why It's Important: In Elixir, processes are independent units of computation. Monitoring these processes helps identify failures and performance issues related to concurrency.

Best Practice: Leverage tools like

Process.monitor/1 and :sys.get_status/1 to monitor the state of processes, track message passing, and identify bottlenecks.

Example:

```elixir
Copy code
```

```elixir
Process.monitor(pid)
:sys.get_status(pid)
```

Use Proper Error Handling

Why It's Important: Elixir embraces the "let it crash" philosophy, where processes are expected to fail gracefully. However, to ensure that the system remains stable, you must use appropriate error-handling mechanisms.

Best Practice: Implement proper error handling and use supervisors to monitor failing processes. Elixir's built-in fault-tolerance mechanisms ensure that the system can recover from errors without crashing completely.

Example:

```elixir
Copy code
try do
  some_potentially_failing_function()
catch
    :error, reason -> Logger.error("An error occurred: #{reason}")
end
```

Leverage Tracing and Debugging Tools

Why It's Important: For complex issues, especially those involving concurrency, tracing the behavior of processes and function calls can help reveal the root cause of a problem.

Best Practice: Use :dbg to trace messages between processes and monitor function calls. This can help identify issues like deadlocks, race conditions, or unexpected behavior in distributed systems.

Example:

```elixir
Copy code
:dbg.tracer()
:dbg.p(:all, :call)
:dbg.tpl(MyModule, :my_function, [])
```

Understand the BEAM VM's Concurrency Model

Why It's Important: Elixir's concurrency model is based on lightweight processes running within the BEAM virtual machine. Understanding this model is crucial for debugging performance issues related to concurrent systems.

Best Practice: Familiarize yourself with concepts like message passing, process isolation, and actor-based concurrency. This will help you debug issues more effectively and design more robust systems.

Use Remote Debugging for Production Systems

Why It's Important: Sometimes, issues only occur in production environments, and debugging locally is not enough.

Best Practice: Use Elixir's remote debugging capabilities to connect to production systems. Tools like IEx can be used to connect to remote nodes, allowing you to inspect the system's state and troubleshoot problems directly in the production environment.

Example:

**elixir**
**Copy code**
**Node.connect(:remote_node@hostname)**

Profile and Optimize Performance

Why It's Important: Performance bottlenecks can significantly affect the user experience and system stability, especially in concurrent applications.

Best Practice: Use profiling tools like :fprof to analyze function call times and identify areas for optimization. Pay attention to the time complexity of recursive functions and the memory usage of processes.

Example:

**elixir**
**Copy code**
**:fprof.profile(:start)**
**:fprof.profile(:stop)**
**:fprof.profile(:analyze)**

3. Leveraging Fault Tolerance and Supervisors

Elixir's architecture is designed with fault tolerance in mind. Understanding how to leverage supervisors and fault-tolerant patterns will help you design systems that recover gracefully from failures.

## Supervisors

Why It's Important: Supervisors are special processes that monitor other processes in Elixir. When a child process crashes, the supervisor decides how to handle the failure, ensuring that the system remains resilient.

Best Practice: Use supervisors to handle failures in critical parts of your system. Choose the right strategy (:one_for_one, :one_for_all, or :rest_for_one) based on your application's needs.

## Conclusion

Debugging Elixir applications requires a combination of powerful tools and best practices. Tools like IEx, Logger, and :observer provide deep insights into application behavior, while the functional and concurrent nature of Elixir necessitates strategies like process monitoring and error handling. By following best practices such as using descriptive logging, isolating tests, and leveraging Elixir's fault-tolerant architecture, developers can troubleshoot and optimize Elixir applications more effectively. With a solid understanding of these tools and techniques, debugging becomes a less daunting task, helping to build stable and performant applications.

## Chapter 14
## Real-World Applications of Elixir

Elixir is widely recognized for its performance, scalability, and fault tolerance, making it an excellent choice for building robust applications in various industries. Here are some real-world applications of Elixir:

1. Web Development

Elixir, combined with the Phoenix framework, powers scalable web applications with real-time capabilities, such as live updates and interactive interfaces. The functional nature of Elixir ensures clean and maintainable code for web systems.

Example: Chat applications, live dashboards, and real-time data feeds.

2. Messaging Systems

Elixir's lightweight processes and concurrency model are ideal for building messaging platforms. Its ability to handle millions of concurrent users without significant overhead is unmatched.

Example: WhatsApp-like messaging systems and notification services.

3. IoT (Internet of Things)

Elixir is used in IoT for managing connected devices and ensuring real-time communication. Its fault tolerance ensures systems remain operational despite hardware failures.

Example: Smart home automation and industrial IoT systems.

4. Financial Services

The reliability and concurrency of Elixir make it suitable for financial services where accurate data processing and fault tolerance are critical.

Example: Payment gateways, fraud detection systems, and trading platforms.

5. Multimedia Streaming

Elixir is used to build streaming services for audio and video, thanks to its ability to manage high loads of simultaneous connections efficiently.

Example: Online streaming platforms and content delivery systems.

6. E-Commerce Platforms

The Phoenix framework allows developers to create fast and scalable e-commerce platforms, enabling real-time inventory updates and seamless user experiences.

Example: Online stores and marketplaces with high traffic.

7. Telecommunications

Elixir, built on the Erlang VM, is an excellent choice for telecommunications systems that demand real-time data processing and high availability.

Example: VoIP services and SMS platforms.

Elixir's reliability, scalability, and developer-friendly ecosystem make it a preferred choice for applications requiring real-time capabilities, fault tolerance, and high concurrency.

14.1 Case Studies

Elixir's unique strengths, such as scalability, fault tolerance, and real-time capabilities, have made it the backbone of several high-profile applications. Below are a few case studies showcasing how Elixir is used effectively in real-world scenarios.

## 1. Discord: Real-Time Communication at Scale

Problem: Discord needed a system capable of handling millions of concurrent users exchanging messages in real time with minimal latency.

Solution: They adopted Elixir for its lightweight process model and scalability.

Outcome: Discord's backend can handle over 12 million concurrent users with sub-second message delivery, providing a seamless real-time experience.

## 2. Bleacher Report: Live Sports Updates

Problem: Bleacher Report required a solution to deliver real-time sports updates to millions of users, especially during high-traffic events.

Solution: By migrating to Elixir and Phoenix, they leveraged the language's concurrency model to handle traffic spikes.

Outcome: They achieved high availability and real-time updates, even during the busiest events like the Super Bowl.

## 3. PepsiCo: Streamlining Supply Chain Operations

Problem: PepsiCo needed a robust system to manage logistics, monitor shipments, and process real-time data across their supply chain.

Solution: Using Elixir, they built a distributed application that ensured data consistency and reliability across multiple nodes.

Outcome: The system improved operational efficiency, reduced downtime, and provided real-time insights into supply chain metrics.

4. Moz: SEO Tooling and Analytics

Problem: Moz required a scalable and fault-tolerant solution to process and analyze large amounts of search engine data efficiently.

Solution: Elixir was used to build their distributed data processing pipelines.

Outcome: They achieved faster data processing speeds and improved reliability, leading to better user satisfaction with their analytics tools.

5. Pinterest: Improving Real-Time Notifications

Problem: Pinterest needed to scale its notification system to handle billions of events daily without latency issues.

Solution: Elixir's concurrency and fault-tolerant processes were leveraged to rebuild their notification infrastructure.

Outcome: They drastically improved system reliability and achieved better throughput, handling billions of notifications with ease.

6. The Financial Times: Real-Time Content Delivery

Problem: The Financial Times required a system to deliver breaking news to subscribers in real time.

Solution: Elixir's Phoenix Channels were used to implement real-time content delivery to millions of readers.

Outcome: They successfully built a fast, reliable system with minimal latency, enhancing user engagement.

Key Takeaways from These Case Studies:

Scalability: Elixir's concurrency model allows applications to handle millions of simultaneous users efficiently.

Fault Tolerance: Elixir ensures applications remain operational even in the face of failures.

Real-Time Capabilities: Ideal for applications that require instant updates or communication.

Developer Productivity: The functional paradigm and clean syntax make complex systems easier to build and maintain.

These case studies highlight Elixir's versatility across diverse industries and its ability to solve real-world challenges effectively.

14.2 Exploring Industry Use Cases

Elixir's combination of scalability, fault tolerance, and concurrency makes it a powerful choice for a variety of industries. Below are some of the most prominent use cases where Elixir excels:

1. Real-Time Communication Systems

Elixir is widely used for building applications that require real-time communication, thanks to its process model and the BEAM virtual machine.

Use Case: Messaging platforms, live chat applications, and collaborative tools.

Example: Discord uses Elixir to manage millions of concurrent users, providing real-time communication with minimal latency.

## 2. Web Development

With the Phoenix framework, Elixir enables developers to create scalable and interactive web applications. Phoenix's real-time features like LiveView simplify building dynamic user interfaces.

Use Case: Social media platforms, e-commerce websites, and content management systems.

Example: Bleacher Report delivers real-time sports updates to its users using Phoenix.

## 3. Multimedia Streaming

Elixir's ability to handle high traffic and concurrent requests makes it ideal for streaming services.

Use Case: Video-on-demand platforms, music streaming services, and live broadcasting.

Example: Companies use Elixir to ensure uninterrupted multimedia delivery with efficient resource management.

4. IoT and Embedded Systems

Elixir is highly effective in managing large networks of connected devices due to its fault tolerance and scalability.

Use Case: Smart homes, industrial automation, and wearable technology.

Example: Elixir-based systems monitor and control IoT devices in real-time, ensuring smooth communication between devices.

5. Financial Services

Elixir is an excellent choice for financial applications that require high reliability and accuracy, such as trading platforms and payment systems.

Use Case: Payment gateways, fraud detection, and real-time transaction processing.

Example: Financial institutions use Elixir for handling millions of transactions without downtime.

6. Supply Chain and Logistics

Elixir helps manage complex logistics operations with its distributed systems capabilities.

Use Case: Fleet tracking, warehouse management, and inventory optimization.
Example: PepsiCo uses Elixir to streamline its supply chain operations and monitor real-time data.

7. Telecommunications

Elixir's roots in the Erlang VM make it a natural fit for telecom applications requiring high availability and concurrency.

Use Case: VoIP systems, call centers, and SMS gateways.
Example: Telecommunication providers use Elixir to manage real-time communication systems.

8. Gaming and Interactive Applications

Elixir powers multiplayer gaming platforms by providing real-time updates and managing high volumes of concurrent users.

Use Case: Online gaming, leaderboards, and in-game chat systems.
Example: Game developers use Elixir to deliver smooth and interactive gaming experiences.

9. Data Processing and Analytics

Elixir's ability to handle large-scale data pipelines makes it a strong candidate for analytics platforms.

Use Case: Real-time data analytics, event processing, and big data platforms.
Example: Companies process and analyze vast amounts of user data efficiently using Elixir.

Key Benefits Across Industries:

Scalability: Seamlessly handle millions of users or devices.
Fault Tolerance: Maintain uptime in mission-critical applications.

Real-Time Performance: Deliver instant responses for high-interactivity use cases.

Cost Efficiency: Optimize resource usage while maintaining reliability.

Elixir's versatility and powerful ecosystem make it a valuable tool for addressing complex challenges across various industries.

## 14.3 Building for Scalability and Resilience

Creating applications that can handle high loads and adapt to failures is crucial in today's technology landscape. Elixir, with its foundation on the BEAM virtual machine, provides powerful tools and paradigms to build scalable and resilient systems.

### 1. Understanding Scalability

Scalability ensures that an application can handle increased workload by either:

Vertical Scaling: Enhancing the capacity of a single machine. Horizontal Scaling: Adding more machines to distribute the load.
Elixir naturally supports horizontal scaling due to its lightweight process model and distributed system capabilities.

Key Features for Scalability:

Lightweight processes that can run concurrently.
Tools like GenStage and Flow for managing workloads.
Easy node clustering for distributed systems.

2. Ensuring Resilience

Resilience focuses on maintaining system stability and recovery in the face of failures. In Elixir, resilience is built into the language and runtime, allowing applications to recover gracefully without interrupting service.

Key Features for Resilience:

Supervisors: Automatically restart failed processes.

Fault Isolation: Failures in one process do not impact others.

Let-it-crash Philosophy: Encourages designing systems to recover instead of trying to prevent all failures.

## 3. Strategies for Scalability and Resilience

### a. Distributed Architecture:

Elixir's built-in distribution capabilities allow you to run multiple nodes that communicate seamlessly. This is useful for load balancing and redundancy.

### b. Fault-Tolerant Design:

Use supervisors and well-defined process hierarchies to ensure failures are isolated and recovered automatically.

### c. Real-Time Features:

Tools like Phoenix Channels enable real-time updates for applications, making them responsive even under high loads.

### d. Load Testing and Optimization:

Tools like Benchfella and ExUnit help in identifying bottlenecks and optimizing performance.

e. Monitoring and Metrics:

Libraries like Telemetry and Observer provide insights into system performance and health.

4. Real-World Examples

Messaging Platforms: Discord uses Elixir to manage millions of concurrent users, leveraging its scalability and resilience.
Web Applications: Bleacher Report relies on Elixir to handle high traffic during live sports events.
IoT Systems: Elixir powers distributed IoT systems, ensuring devices remain connected and operational.

Conclusion

Building scalable and resilient applications is vital for modern software systems. Elixir's concurrency model, fault tolerance, and distribution capabilities make it an excellent choice for handling demanding workloads while maintaining reliability and performance.

# PART VI: MASTERING FUNCTIONAL PROGRAMMING WITH ELIXIR

## Chapter 15
## Functional Design Patterns in Elixir

Elixir, rooted in functional programming, offers powerful design patterns that promote clean, maintainable, and efficient code. These patterns help developers solve common problems while leveraging Elixir's strengths, such as immutability, concurrency, and scalability.

1. The Pipeline Pattern

Elixir's |> operator allows chaining functions for a clear and readable flow of data transformations.

Use Case: Processing data through a series of operations, such as filtering and formatting.

Example:
elixir
Copy code
```
input_data
|> validate()
|> transform()
|> save_to_db()
```

## 2. The Supervisor Pattern

This pattern is fundamental for building fault-tolerant systems in Elixir. Supervisors monitor processes and restart them in case of failures.

Use Case: Managing and recovering worker processes.

Example:
elixir
Copy code
```
children = [
```

```
  {WorkerModule, args}
]
Supervisor.start_link(children, strategy: :one_for_one)
```

## 3. The GenServer Pattern

GenServers abstract server-client interactions, making it easier to manage state and handle requests.

Use Case: Stateful processes like cache, session management, or event handling.

Example:
elixir
Copy code
```
def handle_call(:get_state, _from, state) do
  {:reply, state, state}
end
```

## 4. The Pub/Sub Pattern

This pattern is used for real-time communication where processes subscribe to topics and publish messages.

Use Case: Chat applications, notifications, and event broadcasting.
Example: Using Phoenix PubSub for broadcasting events.

5. The Stateless Pattern

Functions operate solely on input arguments without maintaining any internal state, adhering to functional programming principles.

Use Case: Utility libraries and pure functions.

Example:
elixir
Copy code
```elixir
def calculate_area(length, width), do: length * width
```

Conclusion

Elixir's functional design patterns enable developers to write scalable, fault-tolerant, and maintainable applications. By combining these patterns with Elixir's process model and immutable data, developers can build efficient and robust systems.

## 15.1 Understanding Functional Design Patterns

Functional design patterns are reusable solutions to common software design problems within the functional programming paradigm. Unlike object-oriented patterns, which often revolve around classes and objects, functional patterns focus on immutability, pure functions, and declarative code. In Elixir, these patterns are particularly effective due to the language's functional nature and powerful concurrency model.

Core Principles of Functional Design Patterns

Immutability:

Functional patterns rely on immutable data structures, ensuring that data cannot be altered directly. This makes reasoning about code and debugging simpler.

Pure Functions:

Functions that depend only on their inputs and produce consistent outputs without side effects are central to functional design.

First-Class Functions:

Functions in functional programming can be passed as arguments, returned as values, or assigned to variables, enabling patterns like higher-order functions.

Declarative Programming:

Functional patterns emphasize what the program should accomplish, rather than how to achieve it, making code more concise and readable.

Key Functional Design Patterns

Pipeline Pattern:

A clean way to chain operations where the output of one function becomes the input to the next.

Example: Data processing pipelines.
elixir

```
Copy code
data
|> step1()
|> step2()
|> step3()
```

Higher-Order Functions:

Functions that take other functions as arguments or return them.

Example: Using Enum.map/2 to apply a transformation.
elixir
```
Copy code
Enum.map([1, 2, 3], &(&1 * 2))
```

Recursive Pattern:

Breaking down problems into smaller subproblems using recursion.

Example: Calculating a factorial.
elixir
```
Copy code
def factorial(0), do: 1
```

```elixir
def factorial(n), do: n * factorial(n - 1)
```

Pattern Matching:

Deconstructing data structures and matching specific patterns for concise and expressive code.

Example: Handling different tuples.
elixir
Copy code
```elixir
case response do
  {:ok, result} -> handle_success(result)
  {:error, reason} -> handle_error(reason)
end
```

Currying and Partial Application:

Breaking down a function into multiple functions with fewer arguments.

Example: Creating partially applied functions.
elixir
Copy code
```elixir
add = fn a -> fn b -> a + b end end
add_five = add.(5)
```

```
add_five.(10) # Output: 15
```

Benefits of Functional Design Patterns

Simplicity: Patterns emphasize clarity, reducing complexity in logic.

Reusability: Modular and composable functions can be reused across the application.

Testability: Pure functions and immutability make unit testing straightforward.

Concurrency: Patterns like the Actor Model allow efficient handling of concurrent tasks in Elixir.

Conclusion

Understanding functional design patterns equips developers to write more maintainable, scalable, and robust code. In Elixir, these patterns, combined with the language's strengths, enable developers to solve complex problems with elegance and efficiency.

## 15.2 Applying Patterns in Elixir Projects

Functional design patterns in Elixir empower developers to write clean, maintainable, and scalable applications. These patterns provide proven solutions to common programming challenges and are especially useful for managing Elixir's unique features, such as concurrency, immutability, and fault tolerance. By applying these patterns effectively, developers can create robust systems tailored to their specific needs.

### 1. Pipeline Pattern

The pipeline operator (|>) is one of the most recognizable features of Elixir, making it easy to apply a sequence of transformations to data.

Use Case: Data processing pipelines, such as parsing, transforming, and saving data.

Example:
elixir

```
Copy code
data
|> validate_data()
|> transform_data()
|> save_to_database()
```

## 2. Supervisor Pattern

Supervisors manage process hierarchies and restart failed processes, ensuring the application remains fault-tolerant.

Use Case: Ensuring system reliability by automatically recovering from crashes.

Example:
elixir

```
Copy code
children = [
  {MyApp.Worker, []}
]
Supervisor.start_link(children, strategy: :one_for_one)
```

## 3. GenServer Pattern

GenServers abstract server-client interactions, allowing you to manage stateful processes cleanly.

Use Case: Building caches, event handlers, or persistent connections.

Example:
elixir
Copy code
```
def handle_call(:get_state, _from, state) do
  {:reply, state, state}
end
```

4. Pattern Matching and Guards

Elixir's pattern matching and guards make code more expressive and robust.

Use Case: Handling multiple cases with clear and concise logic.

Example:
elixir
Copy code

```elixir
def process_input({:ok, data}) when is_list(data), do:
handle_list(data)
def process_input({:error, reason}), do: log_error(reason)
```

5. Recursive Patterns

Recursion is used to process collections or solve problems iteratively.

Use Case: Implementing custom enumerable operations.

Example:
elixir
Copy code
```elixir
def sum([]), do: 0
def sum([head | tail]), do: head + sum(tail)
```

6. Higher-Order Functions

Elixir's higher-order functions, such as those in the Enum and Stream modules, simplify working with collections.

Use Case: Applying transformations, filtering, or aggregations on data.

Example:

elixir

Copy code

```
Enum.filter([1, 2, 3, 4], &(&1 > 2))
```

7. Event-Driven Patterns

With Pub/Sub and message passing, Elixir excels in building event-driven systems.

Use Case: Real-time notifications or background task processing.

Example:

elixir

Copy code

```
Phoenix.PubSub.broadcast(MyApp.PubSub,        "topic",
%{message: "Hello"})
```

Benefits of Applying Patterns

Clarity: Makes the codebase easier to understand and maintain.

Reusability: Encourages modular design, reducing redundancy.

Fault Tolerance: Patterns like supervisors ensure the application can recover from failures.
Scalability: Facilitates distributed and concurrent systems, ideal for high-load scenarios.

Conclusion

By applying functional design patterns, developers can unlock Elixir's full potential, creating applications that are efficient, scalable, and resilient. These patterns not only solve specific technical challenges but also contribute to building software that is easy to maintain and extend over time.

15.3 Best Practices for Functional Design

Functional design focuses on creating programs that are modular, predictable, and maintainable by emphasizing immutability, pure functions, and declarative programming. Following best practices ensures that your functional applications are efficient, robust, and easy to understand.

1. Embrace Immutability

Why: Immutable data ensures that functions don't alter shared state, reducing bugs caused by unexpected side effects.

How: Always use immutable data structures and avoid directly modifying variables.

Example:

```elixir
Copy code
# Avoid:
state = %{count: 0}
state.count = state.count + 1  # This mutates the state

# Prefer:
state = %{count: 0}
new_state = %{state | count: state.count + 1}
```

2. Write Pure Functions

Why: Pure functions are easier to test and debug since their outputs depend only on inputs.

How: Avoid side effects and rely only on function arguments.

Example:

```elixir
Copy code
def multiply(a, b), do: a * b  # Pure function
```

## 3. Use Pattern Matching

Why: Pattern matching makes functions more expressive and robust by clearly defining input expectations.
How: Match specific data structures or values in function heads or clauses.

Example:

```elixir
Copy code
def greet({:ok, name}), do: "Hello, #{name}"
def greet({:error, _reason}), do: "An error occurred"
```

## 4. Favor Recursion Over Loops

Why: Functional languages like Elixir encourage recursion for iteration, as it aligns with immutability principles.
How: Use base cases to terminate recursion and handle data incrementally.

Example:
elixir
Copy code
```
def sum([]), do: 0
def sum([head | tail]), do: head + sum(tail)
```

5. Leverage Higher-Order Functions

Why: They improve code reusability and readability by abstracting common patterns.
How: Use built-in functions like Enum.map/2 and Enum.filter/2 to operate on collections.

Example:

elixir
Copy code
```
Enum.map([1, 2, 3], &(&1 * 2)) # Doubles each element in the list
```

## 6. Modularize Code

Why: Small, focused modules and functions are easier to understand and test.

How: Break down functionality into reusable components and organize related functions into modules.

Example:

```elixir
Copy code
defmodule MathUtils do
  def add(a, b), do: a + b
  def multiply(a, b), do: a * b
end
```

## 7. Use the Pipe Operator (|>)

Why: Improves readability by expressing a sequence of operations as a pipeline.

How: Chain transformations and operations on data.

Example:

```elixir
```

Copy code

```
data
|> preprocess()
|> transform()
|> save()
```

## 8. Test Thoroughly

Why: Functional code is easier to test due to the lack of side effects and emphasis on pure functions.

How: Write unit tests for pure functions and integration tests for complex workflows. Use tools like ExUnit for testing.

Example:

elixir
Copy code

```
test "adds two numbers" do
  assert MathUtils.add(2, 3) == 5
end
```

## 9. Optimize for Concurrency

Why: Elixir's concurrency model is one of its greatest strengths.

How: Use lightweight processes and tools like GenServer, Tasks, and Supervisors for parallel execution.

Example:

```elixir
Copy code
Task.async(fn -> compute_heavy_task() end)
```

## 10. Document and Refactor Regularly

Why: Clear documentation and refactoring improve code maintainability.

How: Use @doc attributes for functions and refactor frequently to remove redundancy.

Example:

```elixir
Copy code
@doc """
Adds two numbers together.
```

"""

```
def add(a, b), do: a + b
```

## Conclusion

Adhering to these best practices in functional design ensures that Elixir applications are scalable, maintainable, and reliable. By leveraging the strengths of the functional paradigm, developers can create efficient systems that are easy to debug, test, and extend.

## Chapter 16
## Integrating Elixir with Other Technologies

Elixir's design, built on the BEAM virtual machine, makes it an excellent choice for integrating with various technologies to create powerful, scalable applications. Its interoperability allows developers to seamlessly combine Elixir with other tools, languages, and systems, broadening its applicability across diverse use cases.

1. Interoperability with Erlang

Elixir is fully compatible with Erlang, enabling developers to use Erlang libraries and tools directly in Elixir projects.

Use Case: Accessing mature Erlang libraries for networking, database management, or telecommunication systems.

Example:
elixir
Copy code

```
:crypto.hash(:sha256, "data")    # Using Erlang's crypto
module
```

## 2. Integrating with Web Frameworks

Elixir's Phoenix framework integrates with modern web technologies, such as REST APIs, GraphQL, and WebSockets, to build dynamic web applications.

Use Case: Creating real-time, distributed applications.
Example: Phoenix Channels for WebSocket communication.

## 3. Database Integration

Elixir works seamlessly with databases using libraries like Ecto for querying and managing relational databases (PostgreSQL, MySQL) or NoSQL solutions (MongoDB).

Use Case: Building robust, data-driven applications.

Example:
elixir
Copy code
```
Repo.insert(%User{name: "John", age: 30})
```

4. Messaging and Event Systems

Elixir integrates with message brokers like RabbitMQ and Kafka for event-driven architectures.

Use Case: Implementing distributed, asynchronous communication systems.
Example: Consuming messages from Kafka topics in real time.

5. Microservices and APIs

Elixir supports integration with other microservices via HTTP (using libraries like HTTPoison) or gRPC.

Use Case: Communicating with external APIs or microservices in a polyglot ecosystem.
Example:
elixir
Copy code
HTTPoison.get("https://api.example.com/data")

6. Connecting with Front-End Technologies

Using Phoenix LiveView or REST APIs, Elixir bridges with modern front-end frameworks like React, Angular, or Vue.js for dynamic user experiences.

Use Case: Full-stack application development with real-time features.

7. IoT and Embedded Systems

Libraries like Nerves allow Elixir to integrate with hardware for IoT applications, interacting with sensors, devices, or embedded systems.

Use Case: Smart home automation or industrial IoT systems.

8. Machine Learning and AI

Elixir can integrate with machine learning models by interfacing with Python (using libraries like PyCall) or leveraging external APIs for AI functionalities.

Use Case: Embedding AI-driven recommendations or analytics.

Conclusion

Elixir's flexibility and compatibility make it an excellent choice for integrating with diverse technologies, enabling developers to build innovative, multi-layered applications. Whether used for backend development, real-time systems, or IoT, Elixir excels in delivering robust and scalable solutions.

## 16.1 Connecting Elixir with Databases

Elixir offers powerful tools and libraries to connect and interact with both relational and NoSQL databases. The most commonly used library for interacting with databases is Ecto, which is a database wrapper and query generator. Ecto provides a rich set of features, including migrations, schema definitions, and support for both SQL and NoSQL databases.

### 1. Ecto: The Database Wrapper

Ecto is the primary tool in Elixir for interacting with databases. It abstracts many complex database tasks and allows for building clean, maintainable queries. Ecto supports relational databases like PostgreSQL, MySQL, and SQLite, as well as NoSQL databases like MongoDB.

Key Features:

Schema Definition: Define data models as Elixir structs.

Query Building: Write complex queries with a functional, composable API.
Migrations: Easily handle database schema changes.

Associations: Manage relationships between data entities, such as one-to-many and many-to-many.

Example:

```elixir
Copy code
# Defining a schema for a User model
defmodule MyApp.User do
  use Ecto.Schema
  import Ecto.Changeset
```

```elixir
schema "users" do
  field :name, :string
  field :email, :string
  timestamps()
end

def changeset(user, attrs) do
  user
  |> cast(attrs, [:name, :email])
  |> validate_required([:name, :email])
end
end
```

## 2. Connecting to a Database with Ecto

To connect to a database, you typically configure the connection parameters in your config.exs file and then use Ecto's Repo module to interact with the database. A Repo is an Elixir module that interfaces with a database using Ecto.

Example (Configuring a PostgreSQL database):

elixir
Copy code

```
# In config/dev.exs
config :my_app, MyApp.Repo,
  adapter: Ecto.Adapters.Postgres,
  username: "postgres",
  password: "password",
  database: "my_app_dev",
  hostname: "localhost",
  pool_size: 10
```

Example: Defining and using a Repo module:

elixir
Copy code
```
defmodule MyApp.Repo do
  use Ecto.Repo,
    otp_app: :my_app,
    adapter: Ecto.Adapters.Postgres
end
```
Once the configuration is set up, you can interact with the database using the Repo module.

3. Querying the Database

Ecto provides both query building and query execution through its DSL (domain-specific language), making it easy to write clean, composable queries.

Fetching Data:

elixir
Copy code
```
# Fetching all users from the database
users = Repo.all(MyApp.User)
```

Using Queries:

elixir
Copy code
```
# Fetching a user by email
query = from u in MyApp.User, where: u.email == "test@example.com"
user = Repo.one(query)
```

Inserting Data:

elixir
Copy code
```
%MyApp.User{name: "John", email: "john@example.com"}
```

```elixir
|> MyApp.User.changeset(%{name: "John", email: "john@example.com"})
|> Repo.insert()
```

4. Migrations

Migrations in Elixir are used to manage changes to the database schema over time. Ecto provides an easy way to create, modify, and roll back schema changes. Migrations are stored as Elixir modules and can be run in any environment.

Creating Migrations:

elixir
Copy code
```
mix ecto.gen.migration add_email_to_users
```

Writing Migration:

elixir
Copy code
```elixir
defmodule MyApp.Repo.Migrations.AddEmailToUsers do
  use Ecto.Migration

  def change do
```

```
  alter table(:users) do
    add :email, :string
  end
 end
end
```

Running Migrations:

```bash
Copy code
mix ecto.migrate
```

5. Working with NoSQL Databases (e.g., MongoDB)

Ecto also supports integrating with NoSQL databases like MongoDB through third-party adapters, such as ecto_mongo. This allows you to use Elixir's functional features with non-relational databases.

Example: Configuring MongoDB in config.exs:
```elixir
Copy code
config :my_app, MyApp.Repo,
  adapter: Ecto.Adapters.Mongo,
  database: "my_app_db"
```

## 6. Transactions and Changesets

Ecto provides changesets to validate and cast data before saving it to the database. Transactions allow you to group multiple database operations into one atomic action, ensuring data integrity.

Using Transactions:

elixir
Copy code
```elixir
Repo.transaction(fn ->
  Repo.insert!(%User{name: "Alice"})
  Repo.insert!(%User{name: "Bob"})
end)
```

Changeset Example:

elixir
Copy code
```elixir
changeset = User.changeset(%User{}, %{name: "Alice"})
Repo.insert(changeset)
```

## 7. Optimizing Database Interaction

Database Pooling: Elixir uses connection pooling (e.g., through pool_size) to efficiently manage database connections, especially in highly concurrent systems.

Database Indexing: Indexing frequently queried columns can drastically improve query performance.

Caching: Use caching solutions like Redis or Memcached to minimize database load for frequently accessed data.

Conclusion

Connecting Elixir with databases is seamless, thanks to tools like Ecto. Whether you're using relational databases like PostgreSQL or MySQL, or NoSQL databases like MongoDB, Elixir provides the necessary tools to interact with data efficiently. By embracing features like migrations, changesets, and transactions, developers can build robust, maintainable, and scalable database-driven applications with Elixir.

## 16.2 Integrating with External APIs

Integrating external APIs in Elixir allows you to connect your applications to other services, enabling functionalities such as sending data to remote servers, fetching information from external sources, or interacting with third-party services. Elixir's concurrency model and functional programming paradigm make it a great fit for handling these integrations efficiently, even when dealing with high levels of concurrency and scalability.

### 1. HTTP Clients in Elixir

To interact with external APIs, Elixir provides several HTTP client libraries, with HTTPoison and Tesla being the most popular. These libraries make it easy to send HTTP requests, handle responses, and parse data.

HTTPoison: A simple and robust HTTP client for Elixir, based on hackney. It supports synchronous and asynchronous requests and is widely used for RESTful API interactions.

Tesla: A modular HTTP client for Elixir that offers flexibility and extensibility, supporting various adapters and middleware for requests.

Example using HTTPoison:

elixir
Copy code
```
# Adding HTTPoison to your dependencies in mix.exs
defp deps do
  [
   {:httpoison, "~> 1.8"}
  ]
end


# Sending a GET request
response                                    =
HTTPoison.get!("https://api.example.com/data")
IO.inspect(response.body)
```
Example using Tesla:

elixir
Copy code

```elixir
# Adding Tesla to your dependencies in mix.exs
defp deps do
  [
    {:tesla, "~> 1.4"}
  ]
end

# Creating a Tesla client
client = Tesla.client()

# Sending a GET request
{:ok, response} = Tesla.get(client, "https://api.example.com/data")
IO.inspect(response.body)
```

2. Sending Data to External APIs

In addition to GET requests, you will often need to send data to an API, such as when creating new records or submitting forms. This is usually done via POST, PUT, or PATCH requests.

Example of a POST request using HTTPoison:

elixir

```
Copy code
headers = [{"Content-Type", "application/json"}]
body = %{name: "John", age: 30} |> Jason.encode!()

response                                              =
HTTPoison.post!("https://api.example.com/users",    body,
headers)
IO.inspect(response.body)
```

Example of a POST request using Tesla:

elixir
```
Copy code
# Sending a POST request with JSON data
body = %{name: "John", age: 30}
{:ok,        response}      =        Tesla.post(client,
"https://api.example.com/users", body, json: Jason)
IO.inspect(response.body)
```

3. Handling Responses

API responses are typically in JSON format, and Elixir provides excellent support for parsing JSON through libraries such as Jason or Poison.

Parsing JSON Responses with Jason:

```elixir
Copy code
# Example using HTTPoison
response                                    =
HTTPoison.get!("https://api.example.com/data")
{:ok, parsed_response} = Jason.decode(response.body)
IO.inspect(parsed_response)
```

Parsing JSON Responses with Tesla:

```elixir
Copy code
# Example using Tesla
{:ok,        response}        =        Tesla.get(client,
"https://api.example.com/data")
{:ok, parsed_response} = Jason.decode(response.body)
IO.inspect(parsed_response)
```

4. Error Handling in API Integration

Handling errors gracefully is crucial when working with external APIs. Elixir's powerful pattern matching and error-handling features can help manage common issues such as timeouts, incorrect responses, or server errors.

HTTPoison Error Handling:
You can handle errors with {:error, reason} or by using try/rescue blocks for more complex logic.

elixir
Copy code
```
# Example with error handling in HTTPoison
case HTTPoison.get("https://api.example.com/data") do
  {:ok, response} -> IO.inspect(response.body)
    {:error,   %HTTPoison.Error{reason:   reason}}   ->
IO.puts("Error: #{reason}")
end
```

Tesla Error Handling:

Tesla provides error responses in the form of {:error, reason}, which can be matched and processed.

elixir
Copy code
```
# Example with error handling in Tesla
```

```elixir
{:ok, response} = Tesla.get(client,
"https://api.example.com/data")
{:error, reason} = Tesla.get(client,
"https://api.example.com/invalid")

case response do
  {:ok, response_data} -> IO.inspect(response_data)
  {:error, reason} -> IO.puts("Error: #{reason}")
end
```

5. Working with Authentication

Many external APIs require authentication via tokens, API keys, or OAuth. Elixir's HTTP libraries support adding authentication headers to your requests.

Example using an API key:

```elixir
elixir
Copy code
headers = [{"Authorization", "Bearer my_api_token"}]
response =
HTTPoison.get!("https://api.example.com/protected-data",
headers)
IO.inspect(response.body)
```

## 6. Asynchronous API Requests

Elixir's concurrent nature allows you to make asynchronous API requests using Task or libraries like HTTPoison and Tesla. This helps when making multiple API calls simultaneously without blocking the main application process.

Example of an asynchronous request with Task:

```elixir
Copy code
task = Task.async(fn ->
HTTPoison.get!("https://api.example.com/data") end)
response = Task.await(task)
IO.inspect(response.body)
```

## 7. Rate Limiting and Retries

When integrating with external APIs, handling rate limits and retries is a key consideration. Many APIs impose limits on how often you can send requests. Elixir provides ways to implement retries with backoff strategies using libraries like

ExponentialBackoff or Broadway for more complex workflows.

Using ExponentialBackoff:

elixir
Copy code

```
# Install ExponentialBackoff dependency in mix.exs
defp deps do
  [
    {:exponential_backoff, "~> 0.1"}
  ]
end
```

```
# Example of implementing a retry mechanism
ExponentialBackoff.retry(fn                    ->
HTTPoison.get!("https://api.example.com/data") end)
```

Conclusion

Integrating Elixir with external APIs is straightforward and can be efficiently handled through libraries like HTTPoison and Tesla. By leveraging Elixir's functional features, concurrency model, and powerful error handling, you can build reliable and scalable systems that interact with external services. Proper authentication, error handling, and asynchronous processing will ensure your application handles API integrations smoothly and efficiently, even under high loads.

## 16.3 Bridging Functional and Non-Functional Paradigms

In software development, functional programming (FP) and non-functional programming paradigms (such as imperative, object-oriented, or procedural programming) represent different approaches to problem-solving and designing systems. However, the distinction between the two paradigms is not always clear-cut. Many modern programming languages, including Elixir, blend aspects of both paradigms, allowing developers to leverage the benefits of each when appropriate. Bridging functional and non-functional paradigms can help create more flexible, efficient, and maintainable systems.

### 1. Understanding Functional vs. Non-Functional Paradigms

Functional Programming focuses on functions as first-class citizens, immutability, and declarative programming. It emphasizes the use of pure functions, where the output is solely determined by the input, without side effects. This paradigm encourages the use of higher-order functions, recursion, and pattern matching.

Non-Functional Paradigms (e.g., imperative, procedural, and object-oriented) focus on the sequence of instructions to perform tasks. These paradigms often include concepts like state manipulation, side effects, and mutable data. Object-oriented programming, for instance, encapsulates data and behavior within classes, while imperative programming emphasizes changes to the program state over time.

2. Combining Both Paradigms in a Single System

While functional programming and non-functional paradigms can seem incompatible at first, modern software systems often benefit from the strengths of both. For example:

Imperative Constructs in Functional Code: While Elixir, a functional language, encourages immutability and purity, certain situations may require side effects or mutable state. For instance, interacting with an external system, such as a database or a UI, might require modifying external states or dealing with mutable objects. These actions do not necessarily conflict with the core principles of functional programming. Elixir provides constructs like Agents or GenServer for managing state in a controlled manner within its functional framework.

Object-Oriented Design with Functional Code: Even in a functional paradigm like Elixir, you can integrate object-oriented design principles like modularity and encapsulation. You can structure the system with modules that group related functions, and make use of behaviors to define interfaces, which is similar to how objects define methods and properties in OOP. Functional code can still interact with and manage state through immutable structures while maintaining modular and organized design principles.

3. Use of Side Effects and State

One of the key differences between functional and non-functional programming paradigms is how they handle side effects and state:

In Functional Programming, side effects are often discouraged, and state is immutable. However, functional languages like Elixir allow you to manage state through constructs like GenServers, which encapsulate state in an isolated process and expose controlled interfaces for interacting with that state. By doing so, Elixir offers a way to handle state and side effects while preserving the purity and declarative nature of functional programming.

In Non-Functional Paradigms, state changes and side effects are an integral part of the system. Object-oriented and imperative paradigms often rely on mutable state and shared resources. When bridging paradigms, functional code can provide a controlled environment for managing state, reducing the risks of side effects, while non-functional paradigms can enable more intuitive, mutable state management when required.

4. Performance Optimization: Concurrency and Parallelism
Elixir's functional nature lends itself well to concurrency and parallelism, but performance often requires integrating non-functional programming techniques:

Concurrency in Functional Programming: Functional programming, especially in Elixir, uses lightweight processes to handle concurrent tasks. Elixir's actor model (where processes are isolated and communicate through messages) allows developers to scale applications effectively. Functional programming patterns focus on minimizing shared state, ensuring that processes can run concurrently without interfering with one another.

Parallelism and Data Structures: While Elixir's functional nature makes it easier to reason about concurrent systems, performance in high-load systems often requires non-functional programming techniques such as parallel processing. For example, Elixir's Task module can execute code concurrently, which is an imperative construct within the functional framework. Similarly, using parallel algorithms or dividing large datasets into manageable chunks for simultaneous processing is a non-functional approach to performance that can be integrated into a functional system.

5. Handling Errors and Fault Tolerance

Functional Paradigm: Elixir, as a functional language, makes error handling explicit through pattern matching, ensuring that different cases (including failure modes) are handled in a controlled way. By using constructs like try/catch, raise, or

Error modules, Elixir developers can write fault-tolerant systems while adhering to the principles of functional programming.

Non-Functional Paradigm: Non-functional programming, particularly in object-oriented programming, often involves exception handling to manage errors. While Elixir uses supervision trees for fault tolerance, object-oriented languages like Java use try-catch blocks and inheritance to manage error scenarios. Integrating both paradigms allows Elixir to use non-functional techniques, such as defining fallback mechanisms, for handling errors robustly, without breaking the functional design.

6. Data Modeling: Immutability and Encapsulation

In functional programming, data is immutable, which means that any change to data requires the creation of a new copy. However, encapsulating data for easy access and modification, as seen in object-oriented design, remains a critical feature for building complex systems.

Elixir's Approach: Elixir allows data encapsulation through structs and modules, providing a way to define complex data structures in a functional manner. While the data itself is immutable, the system can encapsulate it in a way that mimics the flexibility of object-oriented systems, where methods can interact with data without modifying it directly.

## 7. Achieving Flexibility and Maintainability

When bridging functional and non-functional paradigms, systems can be designed to be both flexible and maintainable by leveraging the strengths of both paradigms:

Functional Code for Business Logic: Functional programming shines when handling complex transformations, data manipulation, and concurrency, making it ideal for core business logic.

Non-Functional Constructs for Interfacing with External Systems: Non-functional programming paradigms often handle the integration with external systems more easily due to their emphasis on state manipulation, mutable data, and process control. When combined with functional approaches, Elixir can manage this complexity in a scalable way.

## Conclusion

Bridging functional and non-functional paradigms enables developers to create systems that are both expressive and robust. Elixir's flexible functional foundation allows it to incorporate necessary aspects of non-functional programming, such as state management, performance optimization, and external system interaction. By blending the strengths of both paradigms, you can build more efficient, maintainable, and scalable applications that take advantage of functional purity and concurrency alongside the flexibility and ease of managing side effects found in non-functional approaches.